Praise for *The Power of a City at Prayer*

"I believe that *The Power of a City at Prayer* could be used as a catalyst for another 1857 Prayer Revival. This book will not only give you hope for America, but it will inspire you to move in united, extraordinary prayer!"

Rev. Che Ahn, *chief executive officer, The Call International; pastor, Harvest Rock Church, Pasadena*

"I can attest to the extraordinary network that Mac has assembled across ethnic and denominational lines. . . . Mac is considered the 'dean' of urban prayer leaders across the nation."

Dr. Ray Bakke, *executive director, International Urban Associates*

"New York has to be the focus of high-level strategic thinking and ministry if we are going to see successful evangelism take place in North American cities. All eyes are focused on this world-class city to see if collaborative evangelistic initiatives can be planned and sustained. This [book] is not only for New York but also for all the cities of the U.S. and Canada."

Dr. Randy J. Bridges, *national facilitator of city/community ministries, Mission America*

"This book will bring great assistance to so many leaders and others [in the national prayer movement], as it is grounded in a comprehensive vision of Christ's lordship mixed with grassroots wisdom and know-how."

Rev. David Bryant, *founder and president, Concerts of Prayer International*

"[This book] could help give voice to the millions of inner-city Christians who are largely unknown by the broader evangelical world across America."

John Clause, *senior director, World Vision New York*

"Mac Pier has been unusually used by God to organize and lead prayer gatherings for ministries and pastors in New York City. His passion to see revival throughout the entire body of Christ has inspired multitudes to approach the throne of grace."

Rev. Jim Cymbala, *pastor, The Brooklyn Tabernacle*

"*The Power of a City at Prayer* is an important documentation of the synergy among faith-based, governmental and other agencies following the World Trade Center attack and earlier times of great crisis. It also represents a great model for future response to any form of human tragedy—the church united in prayer for renewal, restoration and transformation."

The Honorable Rev. Floyd H. Flake, *senior pastor, The Greater Allen A.M.E. Cathedral of New York; U.S. congressman, retired*

"Pier and Sweeting have shown the awesome power of prayer in the life of people and a city. This book opens up new opportunities for those who have never experienced the incredible work of God through consistent and persistent prayer."

The Honorable Rev. W. Wilson Goode Sr., *senior advisor on faith-based initiatives, Public/Private Ventures; former mayor of Philadelphia*

"This book will inspire you, challenge you and give you hope for how God can transform your city when people of different racial, ethnic and cultural backgrounds come together to pray."

Rev. Dr. Brenda Salter McNeil, *president, Overflow Ministries, Inc.*

"*The Power of a City at Prayer* is . . . the testimony of churches, pastors and business people coming together to 'pray and seek his face.' This book will inspire and ignite your faith to believe God for what can happen in your own life, church and city."

Rev. Luciano Padilla Jr., *pastor, Bay Ridge Christian Center, Brooklyn*

"Through wonderful storytelling about actual people and events, Mac and Katie tell how God honors, blesses and uses those who seek him in prayer. Even the smallest of seeds grows into the largest of plants! This book will revitalize your prayer life and give you practical suggestions and examples on how you can lead and encourage others to come together and pray. A wonderful 'how to' on corporate prayer!"

Claudia Roux, *chief operating officer, Alpha North America*

"Mac Pier truly understands the power of prayer—not just in petitioning God in heaven but in uniting churches on earth so deeply divided by denomination, race, ethnicity, theology, geography, economics and politics. Nothing else has this power. When we are united in prayer, we are united indeed."

Richard Stearns, *president, World Vision United States*

THE POWER OF A CITY AT PRAYER

What Happens When Churches

Unite for Renewal

Mac Pier & Katie Sweeting

Foreword by Ray Bakke

Introduction by David Bryant

IVP Books

An imprint of InterVarsity Press
Downers Grove, Illinois

InterVarsity Press
P.O. Box 1400, Downers Grove, IL 60515-1426
World Wide Web: www.ivpress.com
E-mail: email@ivpress.com

InterVarsity Press® is the book-publishing division of InterVarsity Christian Fellowship/USA®, a student movement active on campus at hundreds of universities, colleges and schools of nursing in the United States of America, and a member movement of the International Fellowship of Evangelical Students. For information about local and regional activities, write Public Relations Dept., InterVarsity Christian Fellowship/USA, 6400 Schroeder Rd., P.O. Box 7895, Madison, WI 53707-7895, or visit the IVCF website at <www.intervarsity.org>.

Cover photograph: cityscape: Mitchell Funk/Getty Images
praying hands: John Turner/Getty Images

ISBN-10: 0-8308-2397-2
ISBN-13: 978-0-8308-2397-0

Printed in the United States of America ∞

Library of Congress Cataloging-in-Publication Data

Pier, Mac, 1958-
 The power of a city at prayer: what happens when churches unite for
renewal/Mac Pier and Katie Sweeting; forewords by Ray Bakke and David
Bryant.
  p. cm.
Includes bibliographical references.
 ISBN 0-8308-2397-2 (pbk.: alk. paper)
 1. Intercessory prayer—Christianity. 2. Interdenominational
cooperation. 3. City churches. I. Sweeting, Katie, 1958- II. Title.
 BV227.P54 2002
 269—dc21

                                                        2002006858

| P | 20 | 19 | 18 | 17 | 16 | 15 | 14 | 13 | 12 | 11 | 10 | 9 | 8 | 7 | 6 | 5 | 4 | 3 |
| Y | 21 | 20 | 19 | 18 | 17 | 16 | 15 | 14 | 13 | 12 | 11 | 10 | | 09 | 08 | 07 | 06 |

MAC:

To Marya, Anna, Jordan and Kirsten,

whose daily lives are an answer to prayer

KATIE:

To my husband, Bill,

my partner in life

CONTENTS

FOREWORD
BY RAY BAKKE

The astonishing new fact of our time is that the majority of the world's six billion people now live and work in sizeable cities. Moreover, we live at the time of the greatest migration in human history. The southern hemisphere is moving north, East is coming West, and everyone is coming to New York! I remember well the day several years ago when, sitting in Manhattan, I read a *New York Times* report that 133 nations had been found living together in one Queens zip code. That is nearly two-thirds of the nations of the world. Professor Saskia Sassen of Princeton asks readers to imagine a gigantic three-legged stool, a colossus of New York, London and Tokyo, which controls huge and growing proportions of the world's resources.

Meanwhile we all saw New York targeted by violence in the drama of September 11. Those images of falling buildings and fleeing people will remain with us for life. But now Mac Pier and Katie Sweeting have provided us with what Paul Harvey would call "the rest of the story," the remarkable drama of praying Christians and churches across the spectrum of New York boroughs and denominations, turning "rubble into revival" in the most amazing ways.

For most of this past decade I have had the privilege of watching Mac and Katie at work up close and personal in the Concerts of Prayer movement. My description of them would be "ministry choreographers." The prayer movement in New York has brought pastors and churches together by the hundreds in retreats and by the thousands in parks and stadiums. They have helped clergy and laity alike to take personal prayer into public settings in ways I had not seen before.

The devotional and missionary literature is replete with descriptions of prayer meetings with protracted hours and thousands of participants in places like Korea or China. But in New York the public prayer meetings look like the gatherings of the United Nations! At Pentecost the church became both international and multilingual, but in New York the public and pastoral prayer meetings are profoundly multicultural as well, from a range of races, languages, classes and denominations that most of us can only imagine.

Yet I have met many of those described in this book. I can attest that New York is being transformed in ways I have not seen in Chicago or Seattle, where I have lived and served over forty years. These are beautifully told stories, organically emerging from powerful biblical texts. I have written for years on the cities in Scripture, but Mac and Katie have taken it to the next level—to the prayers that transformed the cities in Scripture.

Revivals that began in New York have transformed America and the world since the first Great Awakening began in the Dutch parishes of that city in 1726. People like Charles Finney, the Tappan brothers (of gas stove fame) and Sam Mills fanned those flames between 1790 and 1840, as described in books by Charles Foster and others. Prayer meetings in the 1880s in the business community near today's Ground Zero spread to cities around the country and in Europe through the ministry of D. L. Moody and numerous colleagues.

Of course, Katie and Mac expand that history in this book. The point I want to make here comes from my self-confessed identity as an "historical charismatic." I believe our God is still hearing the timeless prayers for New York by that "great cloud of witnesses" who came before our generation in that city. Their prayers join those of today, a co-mingled polychrome cacophony of believers together in the presence of God Almighty, who is responding simultaneously to generations of praying Christians and churches in New York City. Put simply, one generation cannot take all the credit for a transformed spiritual reality in New York, or any other city for that matter. Katie and Mac would agree.

The contemporary stories and biblical expositions in this book would be sufficient to document the impact of prayer in New York, but the book assumes we would also need to know in very practical ways how we can facilitate the Holy Spirit's work among people who would pray in our own cities. I cannot remember a book that brought data and devotion together more effectively. Thank you both, and God bless the Big Apple.

PREFACE

From Farmlands to Flushing

Authors' note: We need to clarify the authorship of this book as we begin. You will find "I spoke" and "my hometown" throughout the book. Yet this book is written by two people. Who is "I" and "my"?

"I" am Mac Pier. When Ray Bakke and I came up with the idea for this book the concepts were clear in my mind. But as I wrote rough drafts of the first chapters, something else became clear: the book would be stronger if someone with greater word skills helped me write it.

My obvious choice was Katie Sweeting, my associate in Concerts of Prayer Greater New York for seven years now. Katie knows me well; she has had urban ministry experience similar to mine; and she is a very good writer. She reworked the chapters, conducted interviews, juggled the outline and generally made this a much stronger book. I thank God for her partnership. This is truly a joint effort.

*　*　*　*　*

My hometown of Avon, South Dakota, has a population of 600, which is fewer people than the membership of my church and fewer than live in the five square blocks in my neighborhood. I grew up surrounded by farmlands—with livestock more plentiful than people.

I grew up with a dual background and a complementary dual prejudice. My mother was a South Carolinian and my dad was a Midwesterner. In my trips to the South I observed a deep mistrust toward African Americans. Blacks and whites worked together in the South, but it was very clear who worked for whom. And living sixteen miles from an Indian reservation, I sensed a mistrust of Native Americans. That mistrust seemed justified as our banking family made many loans to Native Americans and experienced a higher than normal nonpayment rate.

A predictable path for my life would have included following in my family's footsteps by becoming a banker and living in isolation from non-Europeans. But God had other plans for me! My mom had four children in less than three years. My parents modeled an incredible work ethic. My Presbyterian roots laid the foundation for experiencing the saving knowledge of Christ during my senior year in high school. God began honing my leadership skills almost immediately, and I brought several youth groups together and led multidenominational Bible studies.

At the University of South Dakota I became president of the local InterVarsity Christian Fellowship chapter, and in 1979 I attended the Urbana missions convention. At Urbana my wife, Marya, and I responded to Billy Graham's invitation to be available to go anywhere in the world God sent us. While at Urbana, I also picked up a copy of David Bryant's book *In the Gap*. These two seemingly unconnected events changed the course of my life.

January 1, 1980, Marya and I made our first trip to visit New York City. As I gazed out from the observation deck of the Empire State Building I remember thinking, "Either God is in control or we are in big trouble." Little did I know that four years later God would call me to make New York City my home.

We moved to New York to work among college students with InterVarsity Christian Fellowship. We brought a bed, a desk and a dream that God could use two small-town folks to contribute to God's work in New York City. God had already been working in my heart and in my attitudes toward people of color by the time we were invited to live with Bishop Roderick Caesar. For one month this godly African American pastor and his wife opened their home, shared their meals, allowed us to play with their children, and gave us a glimpse into life and ministry in New York City—through their eyes. I began to love the very community I had been taught to distrust, and I gratefully accepted the love extended to me by the Caesar family.

Our journey to New York was also a symbolic journey to reconciliation and healing in my own life. As I experienced the love of God with the whole body of Christ in New York—that colorful and beautiful mosaic—I began to discover my calling as a prayer leader, with New York City as my parish.

Just as I grew up a dual person, in many ways our cities are dual cities: black and white, Protestant and Catholic, rich and poor. The only way to bridge the gaps and heal the divide that exists between churches and between individuals is through a movement of united prayer. Every Christian has a dual membership: in the body of Christ, and in their town or city. United prayer is the most powerful way of experiencing the healing of the body of Christ and seeing the power of God to transform a city. Katie and I offer this book in hopes that it will help Christians in many places start and continue programs of united prayer, so that God will be even more present in our neighborhoods and cities.

Mac Pier

ACKNOWLEDGMENTS

Writing a book is a team effort. A core value for the prayer movement in New York City is appreciating, enjoying and celebrating one another's contributions.

To our editor, Linda Doll, thank you for advocating for us, working with us, encouraging us, prodding us and helping us every step of the way.

To all those interviewed for this book, thank you for sharing your lives: David Van Fleet, Jeremy Del Rio, Glen Kleinknecht, John Clause, Richard Galloway, Rev. Dan Mercaldo, Bishop Roderick Caesar Jr., Rev. David Bryant, Rev. A. R. Bernard. Thanks to Rev. Bill Malick for his movie knowledge and to Bill Barnett for his enthusiasm. Blessings to Rev. Jackson Senyonga for his passion for prayer.

To the Concerts of Prayer Greater New York board of directors, our thanks for their leadership and commitment to the prayer movement vision in which we have invested our lives together.

To our staff team—Beverly, Helen, Alice, Carlos, Brian, Peggy, Roger and Susan, it is a privilege to labor alongside you in the great work of prayer.

To our spouses, Marya and Bill, and our children, Anna, Jordan and Kirsten, and Josh, Tim and Benny, thanks for putting up with laptops on the kitchen table and long days and nights of writing.

Most of all, thank you, Jesus, for inspiring us and for dwelling in our city. May you receive all the glory and the honor.

INTRODUCTION
BY DAVID BRYANT

Standing on the crest of a nearby hill, I watched smoke from September 11 blanketing Lower Manhattan, filling the New York skyline as far as eye could see. It reminded me of the grim funeral pyres I've visited along the Ganges in India. But it also reminded me of a different kind of smoke I've witnessed for years ascending over the Big Apple—the incense of Christians' prayers (as pictured in Rev 5:8) covering a whole city with *hope.*

For nearly two decades, intentional, specific, strategic, concerted prayers have gone up from the heart-altars of hundreds of pastors, thousands of churches and tens of thousands of believers—old and young, of all denominations and ethnicities—from the five boroughs and three states that make up metropolitan New York. Believers and prayer leaders are working for change in their cities, and their work is prayer. *That's why we're here!*

I tell leaders everywhere that *the united prayer thrust in New York City is the most significant urban prayer movement in the world.* That's a hefty claim. But I believe that here in New York any community can learn firsthand what the power of a praying city looks like...and how that power can be experienced anywhere. I believe this even more since the Twin Towers fell.

For example, one thing we relearned last September is that our sovereign Lord Jesus is never caught by surprise. His kingdom economy secured a direct linkage between years of "incense" and the black billows from Ground Zero. Frankly, since those tragic attacks this city has experienced marvelous answers for which Christians have beseeched heaven for a long time. You'll survey some of these answers in the following chapters by Mac and Katie.

WHERE IT BEGAN

Discovering the power of a praying city did not begin for me in 2001. Other dates loom large as well:

• **1970** Pastoring a student-oriented church adjacent to Kent State University, I was driven to convene my elders into weeks of prayer following the infamous revolution on our campus. As a result, the ensuing years saw a *spiritual* revolution in our city as activists from around the nation visited the site of the shootings, only to come to Christ before they left.

• **1980** Working out of the national headquarters of InterVarsity Christian Fellowship, I gathered a group of pastors in Madison, Wisconsin, to resurrect the eighteenth-century Concerts of Prayer movement. We drew Christians across the city into monthly prayer gatherings for revival that extended ten years before my move to New York. Many ministries locally and beyond were birthed. Many Christians were rekindled in their passion for Christ. Unity in the body of Christ expressed itself in fresh ways before the watching city.

• **1984** In Seoul, Korea, nearly 3,000 prayer leaders from 70 nations, representing hundreds of communities, gathered for a week-long International Prayer Assembly for World Evangelization. The first of its kind in church history, it spawned city prayer movements across the globe.

• **1988** The *Prayer Pacesetters Sourcebook* was published, gathering in one volume over 100 major principles for igniting and sustaining urban prayer movements.

- **1994** I invited Mac Pier and his New York team to join COPI, forming our "Urban Strategy Division" (USD). From that point, New York became a "laboratory" in which we could test a variety of tactics for fostering united prayer, plus study directly the kinds of impact such a movement might have on city transformation. Eventually, however, God blessed Mac's efforts so wonderfully that the division outgrew the organization! So we launched it as a stand-alone called Concerts of Prayer Greater New York.

- **2002** The work goes on. We are developing another International Prayer Assembly (IPA II), which, among other things, will provide a "coming out party" for urban prayer movements in many nations. New York will provide a primary case study. Another example: COPI has set in motion a whole new outreach to cities called PROCLAIM HOPE. It is designed to foster in cities worldwide a "Christ-awakening" as the central passion for every church involved in community prayer and transformation efforts. In essence, that's the vision toward which New York has been praying since day one!

GOD'S GRACE UPON NEW YORK

Staring at the horrific destruction in lower Manhattan that day, my mind flooded with memories of—believe it or not—God's *unrelenting grace* upon our city through the multifaceted expressions of united prayers these past years. A few of the events I recalled:

- An all-city leaders' morning prayer gathering at a church in a tough section of the Bronx, where we were guarded by armed watchmen as we met.

- "Prayer booths" set up around the perimeters of Times Square on New Year's Eve, offering to pray with anyone requesting it, and being besieged with lines of New Yorkers desperate for it.

• A team of high schoolers spending all night in Shea Stadium, praying over every seat in preparation for the next day's 40,000-strong Promise Keepers rally, the most ethnically diverse event PK has ever sponsored.

• One weekend when a team of us traveled to eight venues around the city to conduct Concerts of Prayer accessible to every New Yorker who wanted to attend.

• A trip to Korea for African American church leaders, sponsored by local Korean pastors, as a way of encouraging reconciliation when the two races were locked in violence in our city. The vision for this came as these leaders prayed together.

• A consultation at Manhattan's Harvard Club with one hundred church and business leaders where we developed the "New York Prayer Covenant." It has anchored our vision all of these years.

Now can you begin to see why I prize so highly the movement in New York that this book documents? And I haven't even begun to describe for you the powerful prayer strategies implemented in many local congregations. One church, for example, hosts 2,000 people at Tuesday night prayer meetings every week. Another has conducted a round-the-clock prayer vigil for 25 years!

M&M'S

The wonderful models of prayer that this book presents, along with the unprecedented urban outreach that has accompanied the praying, is based on a solid theological perspective that can be summarized by five major characteristics. I call them the "five M's":

Miracle. Just as faith is a gift of God, so is prayer, so are praying people and so is a prayer movement. Nothing in any of us "naturally" wants to seek God's face. Rather, we want to run from him "naturally." What I've described in New York, therefore, is to the Spirit's credit alone. As Dr. J. Edwin Orr summarized his sixty years of scholarly research on revival: "Whenever God is ready to do something new with His people, He first sets them to praying." He has done that for us! He can do it for you.

Message. When our Father sets us to praying, it's because he intends to answer the very prayers he puts in our hearts. So the movement in New York is also a message of *hope* to all of us: his answers are on their way. The "prayer awakening" is actually the *first phase* of the Christ-awakening for which all of us are praying. Christ calls us not only to pray but also to *get ready* for the extraordinary works of God's kingdom that will result.

Ministry. Through the prayer movement, even before all the answers become visible, God is already ministering to us *foretastes* of the revival to come. For example, the movement has created a level of unity among the churches that seasoned leaders who've served here for forty years tell us is broader and deeper than anything known before. Furthermore, out of our praying together God has launched numerous ministries, such as Concerts of Prayer teaming with World Vision/ USA in comforting victims of 9/11. Or take the formation in early 2002 of the Northeast Clergy Association (with the mayor on hand at its inaugural luncheon). None of this would have jelled had we not been seeking God together. Of course, there are *always* huge encouragements for weary believers simply in experiencing dynamic prayer gatherings.

Must. There's no doubt in any of our minds, as we survey the challenges of New York City, that John Wesley was right: "God does nothing but by the prayers of His saints." And Wesley concurs with Andrew Murray, who taught that "God rules the nations [and its cities] by the prayers of His saints." As Ephesians 6 reinforces, once we're armed for the battle we must give ourselves to constant, united prayer (like an army) if we're to prevail over the dark forces arrayed against us. For in the end, the power of a praying city does not lie in our prayers but rather in the Christ who speaks them and seals them through his praying church (see Ps 110:1-4).

Movement. Looking toward the future, I know this flagship for urban prayer endeavors has only begun to set sail. Put another way, we are only in the "outer courts" of a living temple God is building in New York and beyond (1 Pet 2:5). He intends to take this united host of intercessors farther, into the "holies" of what a truly powerful prayer movement should look like anywhere. That's why we call it a *movement.* There's nothing static about it. Day by day, prayer by prayer, gathering by gathering, *we're going somewhere!* Our vision is nothing less than God's answer to the prayer of Jeremiah 33:3, when he promised the prophet his city would "become for me a praise, joy and renown in all the earth" (v. 10).

When (not if, but when) that day comes for New York and the world's other cities, then (and, in a sense, only then) will we truly grasp how potent is Christ's power on behalf of a praying city!

PART ONE

PRAYER
in the
CITY

1

WAS ANYONE PRAYING IN NEW YORK?

On September 11, 2001, the Twin Towers came down. It was a day no one who lives in New York will ever forget. As the terror unfolded live on television, people around the world saw the unforgettable vision of planes flying into skyscrapers. As the World Trade Center came down, the prayers were going up.

The first known intercessor on the scene, Father Mychal Judge, the firefighters' priest, was ushered into eternity as he prayed over a fire-fighter who was killed while rescuing others. Rev. Richard Del Rio arrived at Ground Zero on his Harley-Davidson on that fateful Tuesday morning, supplied with a clergy collar, a police identification tag and an intercessor's heart. As it happens, he was the only pastor on site in those first minutes after the attack. His first prayer assignment was to pray over body parts—that were not attached to a body. Rev. Del Rio was in a constant attitude of prayer as he climbed The Pile, as the rubble became known, aiding in the search for survivors. For days he lived on two or three hours of sleep, returning to The Pile to continue the ministry of prayer.

I was on the fifteenth floor of the Empire State Building at 8:30 a.m. on September 11, preparing for the annual board of directors' meeting of Concerts of Prayer Greater New York. The first board member, Tom Mahairas, arrived in a rush and informed us that a plane had just crashed into the North Tower of the World Trade Center. My immediate thought was that it must have been pilot error. Soon we learned the awful truth: terrorists had attacked New York City.

The board meeting was canceled, and the Empire State Building—once again the tallest building in New York City—was evacuated. As we exited onto Fifth Avenue we saw billows of coal-black smoke rolling up the avenue from downtown. We crossed the street and had an impromptu prayer meeting then and there.

Trying to leave the island of Manhattan was a surreal experience. Dazed and sooty, hundreds of confused and frightened people were walking uptown. Bridges and tunnels were closed, and as we crawled along in the traffic, the news reported the towers collapsing.

At the end of that day, nearly 3,000 people had died, including 300 firefighters. New York City lost more firefighters on September 11 than in all of its previous years combined. One firm with headquarters in the World Trade Center, Cantor Fitzgerald, lost 700 employees. Over 22 million square feet of office space was instantaneously destroyed—the equivalent of downtown Cincinnati. By October, over 80,000 people had lost their jobs.

The statistics are staggering, but they become meaningful when we put faces on them. Two of the policemen killed in the attack were from our local 109th precinct in Flushing, Queens. Their widows and children attended a Sunday morning worship service at First Baptist Church of Flushing in October. The congregation wept at the sight of these victims of the World Trade Center disaster. Many in our city, and even in the church, have asked, "Where was God in all of this? Was anyone praying?"

Mayor Guiliani commented in his farewell address that on no other single day in American history had so many lives been lost and saved at the same time. The horrific tragedy of September 11 claimed almost 3,000 precious lives. But if the attack had taken place a few hours later, or if the towers had tipped over rather than imploding, or if the planes had hit the towers on lower floors, as many as 50,000 could have lost their lives that day. The evil a fallen world inflicts is horrible. But God was very present on September 11, restraining an even more devastating loss of life.

As news of the attack was broadcast, millions of Christians were praying here in New York and across the nation. Churches immediately began opening their doors for impromptu prayer meetings. On Sunday, September 16, almost every church in New York had an influx of lapsed members and visitors. People were seeking God and looking for answers.

The Ground Zero Clergy Task Force emerged in the days following the attack, led by Rev. Marcos Rivera and Rev. Richard Del Rio. This spontaneous coalition of pastors from the Lower East Side convened a prayer meeting on Sunday, September 16. Over 50 clergy and 2,000 people worshiped and prayed at a public park adjacent to Primitive Christian Church, five blocks from Ground Zero.

The American Families Assistance Fund was created by World Vision and Concerts of Prayer just two days after the attack. By the end of December more than six million dollars had been raised to help meet the spiritual, emotional and physical needs of families directly affected by the collapse of the World Trade Center. Applicants received their checks in local churches, accompanied by prayer from the pastor of the church. All of the applicants have been blessed by this arrangement and are very thankful for the financial help. Some have even accepted the Lord Jesus as Savior for the first time.

The Network New York City Coalition convened its first meeting on Friday, September 14. The uniting of more than a dozen of the leading Christian organizations has led to a coordinated response to the tragedy. This coordinated response resulted in the formation of <www.networknyc.org>, a collaborative website to coordinate events and resources in New York City. One of the lessons from September 11 has been the reminder that *we can accomplish much more together than we can alone.*

It is amazing to look back and observe the pace at which coalitions formed and networks united. The groundwork had been laid in the previous fifteen years of united praying in the New York region. Pastors who had prayed together now joined hands in prayer over traumatized rescue workers at Ground Zero. Christian leaders who had prayed together now planned trauma counseling training and memorial services.

Over eighty Christian leaders met on September 24 at the Christian Cultural Center in Brooklyn, New York, pastored by Rev. A. R. Bernard. As a result of that meeting, a memorial service was planned for the one-month anniversary of 9/11. In just seventeen days, satellite technology was in place and dozens of churches had signed up to participate. On October 11, over 10,000 people joined together in prayer at churches across the region, including 6,000 on site at the Christian Cultural Center. The broadcast reached across North and South America.

During the memorial service Rev. Franklin Graham and Rev. A. R. Bernard spoke, acknowledging that all nations of the world had been affected by the attack. They were joined by Howard Lutnick, CEO of Cantor Fitzgerald (a financial services conglomerate), a man still devastated by the loss of 700 employees, including his own brother. Four of the New York Yankees participated via video, and one of the many pregnant widows gave her poignant testimony. Rev. Franklin Graham testified to the certainty of God in an uncertain world.

FIFTEEN YEARS OF UNITED PRAYING

My own prayer life was revolutionized during a trip to Bihar, India, with my wife, Marya, in the summer of 1983. Bihar is known as the "graveyard of missions" and is the birthplace of Buddhism. Bihar is also home to millions of Muslims. Only .02 percent of the population of Bihar are Christians. In that context, we spent ten weeks with missionaries from India, Ireland, England, Scotland and Canada. Each Friday we met to pray. Sometimes we prayed for three hours, sometimes as long as nine hours. I began to feel that sense of utter helplessness that Norwegian pastor O. Hallesby, in his book *Prayer,* describes as the essence of prayer. My prayer life has not been the same since.

In April 1987, Rev. David Bryant led a concert of prayer in Moody Church, Chicago. Shortly thereafter I met with Rick Richardson, on staff with InterVarsity Christian Fellowship in Chicago. He told me of this prayer gathering, which had included a thousand people from every denomination and ethnic background in Chicagoland. I was thrilled with the prospect of a similar gathering in New York City. Wouldn't that be a taste of heaven—to gather all nations in united prayer?

What is a concert of prayer? The phrase "concert of prayer" originated with the revivalist Jonathan Edwards and first appears in his book *A Humble Attempt,* written in 1747. Edwards realized that the body of Christ came together in "visible unity and explicit agreement" when united in prayer. He envisioned all denominations gathering together in united prayer, and for two centuries folk from New England churches gathered quarterly to pray together. United prayer was the sustaining power of the Great Awakenings in New England in the eighteenth and nineteenth centuries.

In June 1987—240 years after Edwards wrote of a concert of

prayer—I met Ted Gandy and Aida Force, who were working with Here's Life Inner City. They also had a vision for united prayer in New York City. As we discussed our shared dream, we began to make a plan. Our goal was to see sixteen churches and two hundred people joined in a concert of prayer in February 1988.

February 5, 1988, was the day. First Baptist Church of Flushing was to be the host church. Flushing is centrally located in Queens, one of the most ethnically diverse counties in the nation. Flushing is home to one hundred language groups; it hosted the 1939 and 1964 World's Fairs; and (as explained below) it is the birthplace of religious freedom in the United States.

At that first concert of prayer there were not 16 churches represented—there were 75! There were not 200 people praying—*500* people gathered in united prayer. God had answered our prayers and exceeded our goals.

By 1989, we held seven simultaneous concerts of prayer on the same weekend: two in Manhattan, one each in Queens, Brooklyn, Staten Island, Long Island and New Jersey. Since 1990, concerts of prayer have been held every first Thursday of May (the National Day of Prayer), with as many as 25 locations and 7,000 in attendance in 1999. In 1999 and 2000 the Greater Allen A.M.E. Cathedral of New York, in Jamaica, Queens, was one of the host sites of the nationally broadcast National Day of Prayer.

THE ROTTEN APPLE AND THE LORD'S WATCH

Marya and I moved to New York City in June 1984. In December 1984 Bernard Goetz, a Caucasian New Yorker, shot five unarmed African American men on a subway. Two months later, as I traveled on a bus in Jamaica, Queens, I realized I was the only white man on the bus. One well-built young black man leaned over and asked me the same question posed to Bernard Goetz on the subway: "Do you have five dollars?"

I was relieved to get off the bus intact. When I relayed the incident to the African American pastors I was visiting, Bishop Roderick Caesar and his father, I expected expressions of empathy. Instead, they howled with laughter. I was getting a small taste of what it feels like to be in the minority.

From 1987 to 1997 a highly publicized story of racial violence occurred almost annually, and each one heightened the tension between black and white people in our city. On December 20, 1986, a black man, Michael Griffith, was killed by a gang of white youths in Howard Beach, Queens. In April 1989 a white woman was brutally raped and nearly killed by a gang of black and Hispanic teens as she went jogging in Central Park. Also in 1989, Yusuf Hawkins, a sixteen-year-old black man, was killed by thirty club-wielding white youths as he shopped for a used car in Bensonhurst, Brooklyn.

Time magazine declared New York City the murder capital of America in its September 1990 issue. By 1992, the murder rate in New York City had peaked at 2,200. Urban violence reached a crescendo in 1992, which was also the year police in Los Angeles were caught on videotape beating Rodney King.

Then God intervened. In April 1992 we experimented with a prayer expression called the Lord's Watch. For one month, thirty churches each took one day and prayed for twenty-four hours over a common prayer agenda. After praying for a solid month for God to pour out his spirit on our region, we saw the jury in the Rodney King trial return a "not guilty" verdict, and the policemen were acquitted. Riots erupted in Los Angeles following the verdict. Given the tenuous racial climate in New York City, would riots erupt here next?

On May 1, 1992, after the King verdict, New Yorkers were panicking and preparing for the worst. Businesses closed early and boarded up. Commuters left work early, piling onto trains, subways and buses. As I rode the subway to the Bronx for the concert of prayer, I was conscious of being the only white man on the train.

New York City was bathed in prayer that day ... and there was not a single outbreak of racial violence. Politicians and newscasters attempted to explain the uncanny calm that enveloped New York City. Why did violence break out in Los Angeles and not in New York City? Ultimately it is a mystery. But there is no better explanation to the restraint of violence in our city than the prevailing hand of God.

In February 1995 the movement called the Lord's Watch was formally launched in New York. The Lord's Watch is patterned after the Moravian Movement, founded by Count Nicholas von Zinzendorf in 1727. Starting in that year, ongoing, uninterrupted prayer began going forth 24 hours a day for 100 years. At least one person was praying every hour of every day, every year for an entire century.

We started here in New York with about 45 churches and 1,000 people. Each church committed to covering one day a month in prayer for four themes: revival in the church, reconciliation between races and denominations, reformation of society, and reaching the lost. The Lord's Watch completed seven years of sustained praying in February 2002, and we look forward to the next seven years with anticipation.

One of the most spectacular answers to prayer since 1995 has been the dramatic drop in violent crime. New York City experienced a 60 percent drop in the murder rate in the 1990s, and it is now the safest large city (of more than one million people) in America. God's people have been praying, and God has been answering.

Dr. Jeff Burkes, the chief forensic dentist for the New York City Police Department, described the morgue as being virtually empty in recent years as compared to the crowding of bodies waiting to be examined in the mid-1990s. Dr. Burkes believes that the policing policies have played a part, but he also believes that only a supernatural cause could explain a drop in crime so fast in a city the size of New York City. The Big Apple is no longer a rotten apple.

> *"Abraham faced Sodom and prayed earnestly for it. We live in a time when God's people are discovering the power of prayer in and for cities."*
>
> RAY BAKKE,
> *A THEOLOGY*
> *AS BIG AS THE CITY*

A MOVEMENT AMONG PASTORS

During the 1990s a spiritual awakening began among pastors in Oregon and Washington under the leadership of Dr. Joe Aldrich. Dozens of pastors attended Pastors' Prayer Summits—96 hours together with no other agenda except to seek the face of God and build relationships with one another. At the summits pastors would pray, worship, repent and take Communion together.

In 1990 we had our first Pastors' Concert of Prayer at Brooklyn Tabernacle. More than 400 pastors participated, traveling as long as four hours to attend. In 1992 we held our first Pastors' Prayer Summit, at the Transformation Life Center in upstate New York, with 35 from diverse racial and denominational backgrounds attending. In 2002, almost 300 pastors from Greater New York gathered for the 48-hour summit. David Bryant has described the prayer movement in Greater New York as the most ethnically diverse and sophisticated expression of its kind anywhere in the world.

In 2001 at our 10th Annual Pastors' Prayer Summit, 200 pastors came together for 48 hours to seek God and build relationships with one another. Many pastors have described the summit as the spiritual highlight of their year, and they look forward to attending the summit each January. In recent summits, prayer times on Tuesday are led by pastors from the Korean American, Chinese American, African American, Hispanic American and European American communities. After sharing the spiritual history and prayer concerns for each community, pastors join together in small groups to pray.

In 1995 two leading pastors reconciled at the summit. Rev. Robert Johansson and Rev. Daniel Mercaldo both lead large churches, and they are two of the spiritual fathers of the city, but they had rarely done anything together. As they knelt and wept together I was reminded of how Jesus must feel about a deeply divided church.

During Communion each evening, Chinese American pastors share the bread with African American pastors, as Latino American pastors share the wine with Korean American pastors. Korean-style early morning prayer is the Tuesday morning wake-up call. Praying in unison, out loud, all together, in all languages, is a powerful experience. At the summit pastors can let down their guard and express their deepest fears and biggest dreams with one another. The unity they share as fellow ministers far outweighs the differences in culture and language.

FOUR CENTURIES OF PRAYER IN NEW YORK CITY

But our present-day praying in New York is nothing new. Believers have been praying here ever since the first settlers arrived to join the Native Americans who had long lived on this land (see figure 1).

The Dutch arrived in New York after the arrival of Henry Hudson in 1609. The Dutch Reformed Church was established under the

The Dutch Century

1500s	1609	1657	1674
Algonquin tribe lives in Manhattan	Henry Hudson arrives	Flushing Remonstrance: religious freedom	The Dutch sell Manhattan to Britain

The British Century

1725	1747	1776	1789
Theodorus Frelinghuysen leads New Jersey revival	Jonathan Edwards starts concerts of prayer	Francis Lewis signs Declaration of Independence	George Washington inaugurated in NYC

The Northern European & Southern Century

1790	1845	1857	1858	1863	1872	1888
Peter Williams founds first black church	Catholic Irish immigrate to NYC	Fulton Street Awakening	Cornerstone for St Patrick's Cathedral is laid	Emancipation Proclamation	McCauley Street Mission	Student Volunteer Movement

The International Century

1891	1900	1915-1920	1939	1959	1965	1988	1991
Ellis Island opens to Southern & Eastern Europeans	Puerto Ricans begin to arrive	World War I	World's Fair	Billy Graham in Madison Square Garden	Immigration Act opens doors to world	Concerts of Prayer movement begins	Billy Graham in Central Park

Figure 1. A Historical and Spiritual Snapshot of Greater New York City, 1600-2000

leadership of Governor Peter Stuyvesant. Governor Stuyvesant imprisoned John Bowne for his Quaker beliefs and released him only after the citizens of Flushing demanded his release in 1648 by writing the Flushing Remonstrance. This document became the cornerstone for religious freedom in the United States.

By the mid-1800s New York City was in trouble. Over 30,000 men were unemployed, drunkenness was rampant, and the nation was divided over the issue of slavery. Then revival came. On September 23, 1857, businessman Jeremiah Lanphier called for a noontime prayer meeting at the Dutch Reformed church on Fulton Street in Manhattan. He advertised the prayer meeting in the local city newspaper. At noon he was alone. By 12:30 p.m., 5 men had joined him in prayer. The following week 14 men showed up. The next week there were 23 gathered to pray. Within two months hundreds of people were gathering for noontime prayer.

The revival that started on Fulton Street spread north to Boston, south to Philadelphia and west to Cleveland. Out of a population of 35 million people, 2 million were converted to Christ in the late 1800s. The prayer meeting led to a revival and culminated in the Third Great Awakening—the beginning of a great evangelical and social awakening.

In September 1862 President Abraham Lincoln signed the Emancipation Proclamation, freeing millions of slaves. More freed slaves came to Christ in the late 1800s than any other ethnic group in the history of the nation. It is no wonder that the African American church is the most important urban institution in the nation.

The social awakening in the mid-1800s is evidenced by the establishment of several ministries to care for hungry and homeless: the Salvation Army, the McCauley Street Mission, the Christian and

Missionary Alliance. The Roman Catholic Church has always played an important role in the social redemption of New York City. Italians, Germans and Eastern Europeans followed Irish Catholics who immigrated to New York in the 1840s to escape the potato famine. Catholic schools and hospitals built in the mid-1800s are some of the most enduring institutions in the city. St. Patrick's Cathedral is the spiritual home to American Catholics. It was the site of numerous funerals for firemen in the wake of September 11.

REVIVAL OUT OF THE RUBBLE?

When Nehemiah was trying to rebuild the wall of the great city of Jerusalem, scoffers thought it was an impossible thing. They mocked the believers: "What are those feeble Jews doing? Will they restore their wall? . . . Can they bring the stones back to life from those heaps of rubble—burned as they are?" (Neh 4:2). But the wall, and then the city, *were* rebuilt—"for the people worked with all their heart" (Neh 4:6).

Tim Russert of NBC's *Meet the Press* has said that the post-9/11 world is in a race against time. Russert claims that we must defeat terrorism before terrorists create the nuclear capability to blow up New York City and Washington, D.C. Saint Augustine reminds us that the city of God is not the city of Rome. Nor is it present-day New York City or Washington, D.C. The city of God is invisible and imperishable. It is time, now more than ever, for the city of God, the church united, to express its citizenship in united prayer and acts of service to a world on edge.

"By the blessing of God, may our country become a vast and splendid monument, not of oppression and terror, but of wisdom, of peace, and of liberty, upon which the world may gaze with admiration forever."

DANIEL WEBSTER

On Saturday, September 15, 2001, David Van Fleet of Street Life

Ministries was attempting to get as close as possible to Ground Zero. He felt called to minister to the rescue workers working on The Pile. On Tuesday, September 12, twenty-four hours after the attack on the World Trade Center, Van Fleet had parked his relief truck at City Hall. His team provided hot soup, hot chocolate, a listening ear and a prayer to anyone who stopped by. After prayer-walking around the perimeter of Ground Zero on Thursday and Friday, Van Fleet was convinced in his spirit God would provide a way for them to move the truck closer to Ground Zero.

As they prayed on Saturday morning, Van Fleet thought about the Fulton Street revival, so he prayed that God would provide a spot on Fulton Street. As they were praying in the truck, a police officer knocked on the door. He asked for a ride and jumped into the truck. They easily passed three checkpoints. The officer got out, and the military guard opened the gate for the truck. Van Fleet describes the experience succinctly: "It was a God thing."

They were directed to park the truck on the corner of Church and Fulton Streets. The officer told David Van Fleet to move to the *exact spot* he had prayed for. When he felt God saying, "Stay here, stay put, don't move an inch," he didn't take much convincing. The truck stayed on the corner of Fulton and Church Streets, ministering to literally thousands of rescue workers, leading many to Christ.

One of the many Christians from around the country who visited Ground Zero in the days and weeks after the attack was Rev. Bruce Porter. He was pastor to Rachel Scott and Cassie Bernall, both killed at the massacre at Columbine High School in Littleton, Colorado, on April 20, 1999. He shared, prayed and cried with the rescue workers and family members for days. Rev. Porter shared with many what God had taught him through the Columbine massacre: "We never see so clearly as when our eyes are full of tears. . . . We never love so dearly as when our hearts our broken. . . . And we never stand so tall as when we are on our knees."

With broken hearts and eyes full of tears, we in New York City are on our knees. We believe, with our brother David Van Fleet, that God will bring revival out of this rubble.

QUESTIONS FOR REFLECTION OR DISCUSSION

1. Where were you when you heard the news of September 11?
2. How did the united prayer in Greater New York City for the previous fifteen years protect the city and prepare the church to respond?
3. Can you identify an expression of united prayer in your city, community or campus?

Next Step: Plan to join the broader body of Christ for a corporate prayer event or celebration on the National Day of Prayer or Martin Luther King Jr. Day.

PENTECOST TO PRAYER MOUNTAIN
The City's Multiethnic Splendor

Walk down the streets of Flushing, in New York's borough of Queens, and the musical strains of Chinese and Korean can be heard. The distinct tones of Asian languages blend with Spanish and numerous Middle Eastern languages. Signs on the stores, restaurants and banks lining Union Street in Flushing are predominantly written in Korean. It's easy to forget you are in New York. English is spoken, but in many neighborhoods it is not the primary language.

My family and I live and worship in Flushing. We have attended First Baptist Church of Flushing since 1984. In our neighborhood, seven out of ten homes are occupied by immigrants. The block we live on is a mini-United Nations, with residents from Korea, Latin America, Afghanistan, Taiwan, Russia and Greece.

To give you a small flavor of the multiethnic nature of my Flushing neighborhood, let me introduce you to three of my neighbors. Two doors down is a Middle Eastern family. This family of six lives in a small two-bedroom apartment. The father was one of the first on the block to put an American flag in his window. He has served as a leader in the mosque on our corner. This same mosque received twenty-four-hour police surveillance for several weeks after September 11 to prevent potential reprisals. This neighbor has often told me that many of his Muslim friends would love to have someone teach them English.

Our next-door neighbors are Taiwanese. The father grew up during the Japanese occupation of Taiwan, and his first language is Japanese. His son, daughter-in-law and grandson live with them—three generations under the same roof. They occasionally attend the Taiwanese Reformed Church.

The corner house is occupied by a man from Greece and his Russian wife; they met during World War II. She attends a small Russian Orthodox church a few blocks away, and their daughter works in the United Nations as a translator. Our block is a microcosm of New York City—diverse in culture, language and religion.

If everyone spoke in their language of birth in our church, more than sixty languages would be heard. That is because 75 percent of our members were not born in the United States. It might sound like the Day of Pentecost! We currently have worship services in English, Mandarin, Cantonese and Spanish. Even the English-speaking congregation is not predominantly Caucasian. One-third of the folks at the English service are of African descent (including black Americans, West Indians and Africans), and one-third are of Asian descent.

The immediate area houses the first Hindu temple built in North America, several Muslim mosques (including a $3.2 million structure built by 200 families), a synagogue, a Buddhist temple, a Mormon church and dozens of immigrant churches. Across the doorpost of the synagogue is written Isaiah 56:7: "My house shall be called a house of prayer for all nations." The 11355 zip code (downtown Flushing) may very well be the most religiously plural zip code in the world. It is a window into the current realities of urban America. I refer to 11355 as "the Soul of Flushing." The nations are truly at our doorstep.

GOD'S PLAN FOR THE CHURCH— A HOUSE OF PRAYER

The Bible begins in a garden, but it ends in a city. The majesty, the grandeur of God can be clearly seen in nature. But God does not dwell only in the mountains; God also dwells in the city. And why not? More than half of the world's people live in cities. In America, 51 percent of all citizens live in just 39 cities. Cities across the country and all over the planet are growing exponentially.

In the last chapter of Revelation one metaphor used to describe the church is that of a city: the New Jerusalem. God does not have a bias *against* cities; if anything, God has a special love *for* the city. Jesus wept over the city of Jerusalem. He weeps over the sin and pain in our cities today. God does inhabit the city.

The New Jerusalem is a city living under the rule and reign of Christ. It is a community of believers. This community includes people from every nation, language and race. There is no racism. There are no theological differences, no geographical biases. This community does not pit blacks against whites, urbanites against suburbanites or Presbyterians against Pentecostals. The walls that we erect so easily to separate us—walls of race, language, region and culture—are all broken down by the blood of Christ. Picture New York City, picture your city, united under Christ. This is what we long for, and this will be the culmination of history—the city of God.

Revelation 5 describes the climax of history as an international prayer meeting attended by people of every nationality and by a hundred million angels. That would fill Yankee Stadium two thousand times! Wow! A multiracial, multilingual, multidenominational prayer meeting—for eternity. Think about that. Wouldn't it be great to get a small taste of that here on earth? In our cities we see the most accurate glimpse of that eternal prayer meeting. When we gather in multicultural, multilingual prayer meetings numbering in the thousands, we are approximating the culmination of history.

Isaiah's vision was to see people of every nation come to God's temple to pray:

"For my house shall be called a house of prayer *for all nations*" (Is 56:7, emphasis added). That verse is often quoted with the last three words omitted. Our churches are to be houses of prayer, but not just houses of prayer for those who look and speak just like we do. Our churches are destined to be houses of prayer *for all nations*.

The great theme of Isaiah 56 is inclusion. Praise God, he is a God of inclusion! The Lord says to the people, through the prophet Isaiah, "Don't turn away the foreigners and their children. Don't put walls around your country and try to keep all the immigrants out. Don't exclude the eunuchs" (who were despised in Jewish society). Who are the people we exclude from our houses of worship today? God is clearly saying, "Let them in. Let everyone in!" And as we let them in, the place of unity is in the house of prayer.

Jesus forcefully reminded the Jews of this verse when he threw the moneychangers out of the temple. They arrived at Jerusalem. Immediately on entering the temple, Jesus started throwing out everyone who had set up shop there, buying and selling. He kicked over the tables of the bankers and the stalls of the pigeon merchants. He didn't let anyone even carry a basket through the temple. And then he taught them, quoting this text:

Is it not written:
　"My house will be called
　a house of prayer for all nations"?
But you have made it "a den of robbers." (Mk 11:17)

Rather than provide an inviting opportunity for foreigners to come to the temple, the moneychangers were manipulating people with the economic gouging practices of selling sacrifices. The temple, the church, is destined to be a house of prayer for all the nations. In Jesus' day, the temple, the meeting place of believers, had been detoured from its destiny. It had strayed from its intended purpose. Our churches today are destined to be houses of prayer for all nations. Let's not get detoured.

THE DAY OF PENTECOST—THE CHURCH BEGAN IN A PRAYER MEETING

The church was born in a prayer meeting. The first two chapters of the book of Acts chronicle the beginning of the church. After Jesus ascended into heaven, the disciples, Mary and the women gathered in an upper room for a prayer meeting. There were about 120 people in all. Jesus had given his disciples one command. He simply told them to stay in Jerusalem and wait for God's promise to be fulfilled.

During that waiting period he wanted them to reconcile their differences. Peter had denied the Lord. Thomas had doubted the Lord. The disciples had abandoned the women. If there had ever been a group of people who had good reason to hate each other, it was this group.

During that waiting he wanted them to pray together, and they did. The Bible clearly says that they were united—through prayer. "These all continued with one accord in prayer and supplication" (Acts 1:14 NKJV). This was the power of prayer to unify believers in action.

On the Day of Pentecost—the Feast of the Harvest—in the midst of their prayer meeting, the Holy Spirit came down. A violent, rushing, mighty wind swept through the meeting place; tongues like fire rested on each one of them (Acts 2:2-3). It was a dramatic moment in history—the church was being birthed.

John Stott points out that "on the day of Pentecost the whole world was there in the representatives of the various nations. Nothing could have demonstrated more clearly than this the multiracial, multinational, multilingual nature of the kingdom of Christ."[1] Each listener heard the gospel proclaimed in his or her own language. More than 3,000 were baptized into the early church in one day.

PAUL PREACHES—AND PRAYS—IN CITIES

Luke the Gospel writer chronicles the growth of the early church in the book of Acts. The good news of Jesus Christ was proclaimed throughout the major cities of the known world. Paul had a God-given missions strategy. He traveled as he was led by the Holy Spirit—and he went primarily to large cities. John Stott confirms that "it seems to have been Paul's deliberate policy to move purposefully from one strategic city-centre to the next."[2] These strategic ports and urban centers served as launching pads from which the gospel could spread to the surrounding villages and countryside. As Paul traveled between Asia and Europe he visited such urban centers as Antioch, Corinth, Athens and Ephesus. The composition of the church was African, Jewish and European. The citizens of Antioch did not know what to call this eclectic group of people whose faith in Jesus the Christ transcended their ethnicity, so they called them Christians.

Paul spent over two years in Ephesus in the mid-50s A.D. Ephesus was arguably the most important city in Asia Minor (present-day Turkey). About 500,000 people lived and worked in this harbor city on the edge of the Aegean Sea. By preaching in Ephesus (see Acts 19), Paul was able to impact every major segment of culture: religious, academic, medical, economic and political.

Paul started his ministry in the synagogue, arguing and pleading with the religious leaders, influencing the *religious community* in Ephesus. Paul then moved to the lecture hall of Tyrannus. Every day for two years he discussed the gospel with the professors and students, thus influencing the *educational community* in Ephesus. Paul also performed healing miracles, affecting the *medical community.*

Ephesus was home to the temple of Diana, a building that was one of the seven wonders of the ancient world. Many Ephesians who worshiped the Roman goddess Diana came to faith in Christ and confessed their sin. When they heard the gospel, they brought their scrolls (books with magical formulas and incantations) and burned them publicly. The value of the destroyed scrolls was 50,000 silver coins, each coin equal to a day's wages. The silversmiths complained about their decreased business; silver shrines to Diana were no longer in demand. Thus, the *economic community* of Ephesus was influenced with the gospel.

When Paul's preaching nearly incited a riot, the officials of the province tried to persuade Paul to keep a low profile, and the city clerk was forced to address the crowd and calm them down. Even the *political community* was influenced by the gospel.

After many trials and tribulations, both literal and figurative, Paul eventually reached the great city of Rome, his ultimate destination. Rome was to the first century what New York is to the twenty-first century. It was the most powerful city ever built—the capital and symbol of the Roman Empire. Rome was the locus of government and technology. Its culture was advanced, its infrastructure was ambitious and efficient, its buildings were world class, and it was the commerce center of the known world. Sounds a bit like present-day New York, doesn't it?

The New Testament chronicles the spread of the gospel from Jerusalem, the religious capital of the world, to Rome, the political capital of the world. From Jerusalem and Rome, the gospel spread throughout the first-century world. In the twenty-first century, the nations of the world are coming to New York and other large cities. The opportunity to spread the gospel has never been greater.

GOD'S PATTERN TODAY: MULTIETHNIC MANIFESTATIONS OF THE CHURCH

Churches generally reflect the makeup of their neighborhood, and since many neighborhoods are homogeneous, many churches are as well. On the other hand, some churches are ethnically diverse. Both models can be glorifying to God, but it is precisely because so many churches are homogeneous that there is a great need for churches to join together in united prayer. Only by joining together with other churches will most Christians experience the joy of praying with Christians from other cultural and ethnic backgrounds. The following is a brief historical summary of some of the ethnic churches in our country. It is by no means an exhaustive list, but is meant to introduce you to some of the ethnic churches God has raised up in America.

THE AFRICAN AMERICAN CHURCH

Africans were kidnapped from their homeland, shackled and chained, crammed into the bellies of ships and brought to the shores of America more than three hundred years ago. The black church that emerged during the horrible days of slavery has become, in the words of George Barna, the most important urban institution in America.

The first uniquely African American church began in 1787. Until then, slaves used the "slave balcony" in the white church. The color line was drawn at the Communion table, in the pews and at the baptismal font. Black parishioners were not allowed to be in close proximity to whites.

Rev. Richard Allen, Rev. Absalom Jones and other black worshipers were kneeling in prayer in St. George's Methodist Episcopal Church in Philadelphia, Pennsylvania, when Rev. Jones was pulled from his knees, and the black worshipers were told to leave.[3] Rev. Allen led the procession out of the church, and what emerged from this ejection was the African Methodist Episcopal (A.M.E.) Church. Peter Williams founded the first African American church in New York City in the late 1790s.

Just five denominations claim 80 percent of all African American church members. The National Baptist Convention comprises the largest number of people of African descent in a single membership body in the world. The other four denominations are Progressive National Baptist, African Methodist Episcopal, African Methodist Episcopal Zion and Church of God in Christ.

In addition to these large denominations, there are huge numbers of independent Pentecostal churches, ranging from small storefront churches to churches with membership in the thousands. While the denominational churches have historically been more politically active, the Pentecostal churches have focused more on personal salvation and personal piety.

The African American community is tragically unique in American experience. It is the largest segment of the population that arrived in the United States against its will. Many immigrants land on the shores of America in search of freedom and prosperity. Africans landed in terror and trembling, longing for home. The crucible of slavery has uniquely shaped the soul of the African American church. From the pit of injustice, African American churches developed a prayer style that encompasses extended days of prayer and early morning prayer meetings.

During the civil rights movement, African Americans often went from their knees in prayer to their feet in protest in cities across the nation. The African American church has understood the unique and vital relationship between the biblical characters Ezra, Nehemiah and Esther. There has always been a need for people like Ezra to build the temple, people like Nehemiah to pray and rebuild the city, and men and women like Esther to change the law.

For years Concord Baptist Church of Brooklyn has held the distinction of being one of the largest Protestant churches in the United States. Under the leadership of Rev. Gardner Taylor, Concord Baptist developed a distinct commitment to children and the elderly. The church started a school, formed a seniors' ministry and established the Christ Fund—a foundation that has raised over a million dollars for compassionate ministries. Over a thousand members have attended Concord Baptist for more than forty years. Gardner Taylor, named by one Harlem pastor as "the best preacher ever born, alive, or yet to be born," was a contemporary of Dr. Martin Luther King Jr. and an important ally in the civil rights movement.

In addition to a large African American population in America's urban centers, it is important to acknowledge the large population of Christians who are first-generation Africans and Caribbean Americans. Many British citizens are also of African descent. God has brought the beautiful variety of Africans dispersed around the world to live in our urban centers.

THE HISPANIC CHURCH

The fastest-growing churches in most urban areas are Hispanic churches. It is estimated that within fifteen years the Latino population will grow to more than 40 percent of the population of California. Nearly two million Hispanics reside in New York City. In 1990, 60 percent of the Latino population was Puerto Rican. The makeup of the Latino community has undergone significant changes during the past decade. Twenty percent of all immigrants during the 1990s were from the Dominican Republic. They created a community of 400,000 Dominicans in Washington Heights, Manhattan. Bonded by a common language, the Hispanic community is amazingly diverse—Mexicans, Cubans, Puerto Ricans, Ecuadorians, Dominicans, Nicaraguans and others.

Following the 1906 Azusa Street Revival near Los Angeles, Pentecostalism spread to the island of Puerto Rico. Large numbers of immigrants arrived in New York City from the island of Puerto Rico at the turn of the twentieth century. Immigrants tend to move near to fellow nationals. Thus, the Hispanic map of New York City reveals large numbers of Puerto Ricans in the Bronx, Spanish Harlem and Brooklyn. Washington Heights is home to a large Dominican community. Many Cubans have made Jersey City their home. Colombians and other Central Americans are found throughout Queens.

While there are many types of denominational churches in Metro New York City, the majority of Spanish churches are Catholic and Pentecostal. Spanish Catholics comprise nearly 50 percent of the Catholic church in New York City. As of 2002, there are more than 1,500 Hispanic churches in the Greater New York area. The vast majority of Hispanic churches hold their services in Spanish. A few Hispanic churches have bilingual services in English and Spanish, to cater to the second generation and younger members.

The Hispanic church is a powerful force on the urban landscape. In 1984, Hispanic leaders in New York and New Jersey launched a Spanish-speaking Christian radio station, Radio Visión, in Paterson, New

Jersey. The station has reached into Cuba and Latin America, and it boasts a daily audience of 500,000. Radio Visión has been a platform to mobilize Spanish Christians on very short notice to participate in citywide events at Madison Square Garden. In just one month, Spanish churches organized a prayer service on Randall's Island for 13,000 people.

Hispanic churches traditionally hold all-night prayer services. At Bay Ridge Christian Center, people are praying twenty-four hours a day. They have seen a tremendous response to the gospel, as dozens of people come forward at weekly altar calls.

Many Hispanic churches link their prayer emphasis to social ministry. One of the spiritual mothers of the Spanish church in New York City, Mama Leo, worked for decades in the prisons and streets of New York City. One of the many men and women she led to Christ was Jerry Kaufman. Bishop Kaufman planted one of the first English-speaking Puerto Rican churches in New York City.

THE KOREAN CHURCH

Koreans began to immigrate to the United States in large numbers after the passing of the Immigration Act in 1965. Nearly 20,000 Koreans immigrated annually beginning in 1973. The 1990 census indicated Koreans to be the fourth largest Asian immigrant group after the Chinese, Filipino and Japanese.

Since 1965 more than 300 Korean churches have been established in Northern Queens, New York City, and 600 in the Greater New York area. A majority of Koreans are Presbyterians, but there is also a significant number of Korean Baptist and charismatic churches. As many as 50 percent of all Asian immigrants are Christian, due to the large number of Christian Koreans who immigrate.

The Korean church was transformed by the suffering it endured under Japanese rule and later on under communism. Many Christians were martyred during the Korean War when the communists invaded South Korea.

Almost all first-generation Korean churches hold early morning prayer that begins at 5:00 or 5:30 a.m., something for which these churches are known. A Korean prayer meeting often begins with corporate worship, and then the pastor delivers a meditation. With God as the focal point of the service, prayer time ensues with simultaneous prayer in which people pray as loud and fervently as they know how. Koreans often go away for days to "prayer mountains"—personal retreats where one can spend long seasons alone with God.

The prayer style of a Korean-speaking church is shaped by the people's experience of suffering as well as by the model of Jesus rising up early to go to a quiet place to pray. Koreans pray with great fervency whether they are Presbyterian, Baptist or charismatic.

The younger generation, however, tends to find the first-generation church boring, and great numbers of young people leave the church as soon as they are old enough.

THE CHINESE CHURCH

Globally, the Chinese church is one of the largest in the world. Church growth in China is one of the most remarkable stories in the history of Christendom in light of the expulsion of Western missionaries and the brutality of communism. However, in the United States, the Chinese church is smaller than the Korean church.

Like the Korean church, the Chinese church is losing its children. As many as 90 percent of children growing up in the church leave it when they reach adulthood. The Chinese church is also marked by an absence of Chinese pastors in the pulpits of its English-speaking congregations.

Many first-generation churches were begun in Chinatown, where the concentration of Chinese immigrants first settled. In New York City, Chinatown in Manhattan has been described as the largest enclave of immigrants in the Western world. In total, there are approximately 140 Chinese churches in Metro New York City.

There have been some efforts to bring the Chinese churches together. An initiative called PaLM (Pastoral and Lay Ministry), headed by Rev. Howard Chan, provides networking, training and outreach opportunities for second-generation Asian American churches. In the past year an effort has been made to bring second-generation Asian American pastors together for monthly fellowship meetings.

Prayers of the Chinese church focus largely on the needs of immigrants and youth. There are tens of thousands of immigrants working in restaurants, sweatshops and laundries. They are overworked and underpaid, working seven days a week for less than minimum wage. Immigrant youth often gravitate toward ruthless Asian gangs. Churches are attempting to both pray for and intervene in the lives of these youth.

THE EUROPEAN AMERICAN CHURCH

It is hard to summarize a diverse group like European Americans. The majority of European American churchgoers are Catholic. In 1990, 43 percent of the people in New York City were Catholic. New York became a Catholic city after waves of immigrants came from Ireland, Germany and Southern Europe between 1845 and 1910. By the end of the nineteenth century, once starving Irish immigrants had built the second most famous church in the world, St. Patrick's Cathedral.

Catholics like Lee Stuart of the South Bronx Churches (SBC) have successfully built powerful coalitions of Catholic and Protestant churches that have transformed their communities. SBC has built hundreds of homes as well as a state-of-the-art high school, The Leadership Academy. Even though The Leadership Academy is located in one of America's poorest congressional districts, a full 100 percent of its first graduating class was accepted into college. The SBC built its coalition by forging long-term relationships with many diverse churches that share the same values.

Waves of renewal have visited the Episcopal church in recent years. One of the primary reasons is the Alpha movement, a program begun by a church in England. Alpha's strategy combines home fellowship with structured gospel messages. All types of denominations are now utilizing Alpha in Great Britain, across the United States and around the world. God has used the Alpha program to bring many people into the kingdom. Alpha's U.S. offices are located in lower Manhattan.

When Redeemer Presbyterian Church was planted in Manhattan, thousands of Presbyterians were praying for its success. In just twelve years, the church has grown from a Bible study of fifteen to a congregation of nearly 4,000. During this time period, Redeemer has also helped start ten new churches.

MULTIETHNIC SPLENDOR

It is impossible to summarize in one chapter the breadth of the ethnic beauty of the body of Christ in urban America. The snapshots provided here offer a glimpse into how God is at work in the African American, Hispanic American, Korean American, Chinese American and European American communities of faith. In some churches the traditions overlap as people of different colors become one church family. Undoubtedly, the landscape of the urban church in America is the most internationally, racially and ethnically diverse expression of the church in history.

God has made us all of one blood to inhabit the whole earth, as Paul told the people of the great city of Athens (Acts 17). In today's cities we have the unparalleled opportunity to participate in this miracle of God. We celebrate and dimly reflect that final prayer meeting described in the book of Revelation, when every nation, language and culture will be represented before his throne. We have the privilege of learning from and loving God's people in our midst.

In our cities today, the diversity of the international body of Christ is a very present reality. In May 2001, I led a concert of prayer in the city hall in Norwalk, Connecticut. Seven hundred Christians from every part of the world filled the building, and their prayers ascended to the throne of grace. I thought of the words Dwight Moody spoke as he saw college students at Cambridge University responding to the gospel over a hundred years ago: "This is enough to live for."

QUESTIONS FOR REFLECTION OR DISCUSSION

1. Identify one area of the Spirit's movement in an ethnic or denominational group that was new to you in this chapter.
2. Can you identify an immigrant or ethnic minority church different from your own that has moved into your community in the past five years?
3. What would you like to see happen in your church that could connect others to the breadth of the body of Christ racially and denominationally?

Next Step: Initiate a meeting with a person from another tradition or background.

3

FIVE DIMENSIONS OF PRAYER

Step through the front doors of Christian Life Church in Kampala, Uganda, at any time of the day or night and you will find people praying. Pastor Jackson Senyonga leads this congregation of 20,000. They have made prayer a priority in their personal lives, in the life of their church, in the city of Kampala and in Uganda as a nation. Imagine that: nonstop prayer. Twenty-four hours a day, seven days a week—including holidays—there are people on their knees crying out to God in prayer.

Pastor Senyonga has said that when one group is at the end of its praying time, they don't let up until the incoming group has gotten "up to speed" in prayer. As a new group of prayer warriors arrives at the church, the baton of prayer is passed off, and intercession continues unending from morning till night. What a wonderful picture of the church at prayer.

AN APPETITE FOR PRAYER

Their prayers are not halfhearted or lackadaisical. They are prayers of desperation. They are not falling asleep at 2:00 in the morning but are continuing to cry out to God—for his presence, for healing, for purification, for deliverance. Indeed, having gone through decades of repression under a series of harsh dictators who would slaughter whole villages for no apparent reason, they have learned to cry out to God.

Pastor Senyonga recently posed this question to a group of pastors from the New York metropolitan region: "America, how do you want revival?" We lost almost 3,000 people in one day on 9/11, but in many nations in Africa 3,000 people die every week of AIDS. Pastor Senyonga believes that revival comes either from passion or from persecution. Uganda is now experiencing a glorious revival, but they arrived at their desperation for God through devastation.

Granted, we in America have not endured the kind of violence and loss that Ugandans have suffered. However, in order to engage in prayer that changes lives, that changes cities, that changes nations, it is necessary to increase our appetite for prayer. As difficult as most of us find it to miss a meal, that's just how difficult it should be to miss our prayer time. If only our appetite, our hunger, for prayer was as intense as some of our other hungers in this society! America would not be the same.

How many of us find it difficult to block out even ten to fifteen minutes for prayer every day? Pastor Senyonga encourages everyone in his church to personally pray for one hour a day! And he leads by example. Knowing people's frailties, and accepting that people come to prayer with different levels of experience and expectation, Pastor Senyonga urges his members to start with fifteen minutes of prayer daily and work their way up to the full hour of daily prayer. This may seem impossible or unrealistic with your schedule. Rise a little earlier, turn off the television a little sooner or make your phone conversation a little shorter. You get the idea. Making prayer a priority will not just bless you or your family and church; it may even bless your entire city!

FOUR PREREQUISITES FOR POWERFUL PRAYER

Pastor Senyonga outlines four prerequisites for powerful prayer.[1]

1. Prayer must be desperate. We must see our own need for God—our utter dependence on him—and cry out to him from our own impotence. Only when we realize that we can do nothing of value without him will we come to him in desperation. May we cry out to God like David:

> I cry to you, O LORD;
>> I say, "You are my refuge,
>> my portion in the land of the living."
> Listen to my cry,
>> for I am in desperate need. (Ps 142:5-6)

2. Prayer must be united. We need to pray in our own prayer closets, in solitude at home, but we also need to pray together. There is no power on earth more potent than united prayer. Jesus told his disciples, "If two of you on earth agree about anything you ask for, it will be done for you by my Father in heaven. For where two or three come together in my name, there am I with them" (Mt 18:19-20).

3. Prayer must be sustained. Prayer is not a practice that we pick up today and drop tomorrow in favor of some new spiritual fad. Prayer is essential to our lives as spiritual beings. Prayer must be a day-by-day practice, sustained on a personal level and also on a corporate level. David urges us to "look to the LORD and his strength; seek his face always" (Ps 105:4). Paul exhorts believers in Ephesus to "pray in the Spirit on all occasions with all kinds of prayers and requests. With this in mind, be alert and always keep on praying for all the saints" (Eph 6:18).

4. Prayer must be inspired. The Holy Spirit inspires our praying, and we need to listen to the leading of the Spirit as we pray. Paul instructs the believers in Rome: "In the same way, the Spirit helps us in our weakness. We do not know what we ought to pray for, but the Spirit himself intercedes for us with groans that words cannot express" (Rom 8:26).

FIVE DIMENSIONS OF POWERFUL PRAYER

Once we have begun to comprehend and embrace the four prerequisites of powerful prayer, we can implement this kind of praying in each of the five dimensions of prayer (see figure 2). The five dimensions are geographically concentric: start with yourself and move outward.

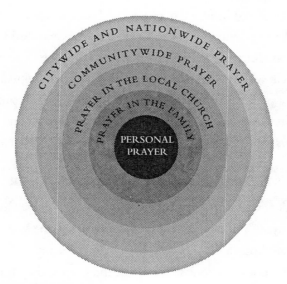

Figure 2. Dimensions of Prayer

Each of these five dimensions of prayer has its own unique rhythm.

- Personal prayer is something we do daily, maybe even hourly.
- Family prayer is done daily or several times a week.
- Prayer in the church is most often done weekly.
- Communitywide prayer is optimally scheduled monthly, but in many communities it may be less frequent.
- Citywide prayer is most often planned yearly, often on the National Day of Prayer, which always falls on the first Thursday in May. National prayer gatherings are held annually; on the National

Day of Prayer local churches have the option to join the nationally broadcast concert of prayer by satellite. Other national prayer gatherings have been held in recent years, but not an annual basis.

For example, on Saturday, October 4, 1997, Promise Keepers convened a massive gathering in Washington, D.C., on the National Mall. Hundreds of thousands of men participated in Stand in the Gap: A Sacred Assembly of Men, a day of personal repentance and prayer.

In all of our praying, we need to understand that God is the One who takes the initiative in our praying. He is the One who is drawing us to himself; we are not initiating the dialogue. It is helpful to keep a journal or a prayer diary, so that you can look back from time to time to be reminded of how God has drawn you to himself and answered your prayers.

THE FIRST DIMENSION: PERSONAL PRAYER

Prayer leaders with integrity have strong personal prayer lives. Pastor Jackson Senyonga doesn't tell his members to pray one hour a day and not pray one hour a day himself. He leads by example. The life of a prayer leader does not consist merely of the prayers they lead in front of the church or in large prayer gatherings. Prayer is an integral part of their inner lives. Anyone who desires to have a leadership role in prayer needs to make personal prayer a high priority.

Personal prayer has two essential components: listening and speaking. Listening can include reading the Scriptures and meditating on a passage, quieting yourself before God and allowing him to speak to your spirit, meditating on the attributes of God or going outdoors and observing God in his magnificent creation. A passage on the awesome power of God is made alive as you gaze out at the stars, the ocean, the mountains or a flower—or listen to the beating of your own heart.

The most important aspect of listening is having a receptive attitude and an open spirit. Although ideally listening is done in a quiet place, it is not always possible to find a quiet place for personal prayer. I love the story of Susanna Wesley, the mother of John and Charles Wesley and seventeen other children. When she wanted to spend time alone with God, she simply lifted up her apron and put it over her head! She thus created a place to meet with God, even in the midst of hectic and noisy family life.

I have found journaling to be helpful in my personal devotions. Writing down my prayers helps me focus on God and gives structure to my thoughts. It also provides a permanent record of my praying; when I review my prayer journals later, I rejoice at how God has been at work in my life. Christian author Ken Gire describes a method of journaling in his book *Reflections on Your Life Journal*. Gire believes that God speaks in everyday moments and that, if we are receptive, we can hear the voice of God through many mediums: a movie, a dream, a conversation, a newspaper article, a song, a painting and so on.

Gire outlines a process for discerning the voice of God in everyday life:[2]

• *Read the moment.* When you feel God is speaking to you, stop and write down what happened. It could be through a sermon or song; it could be an article you read or a scene you pass on the street. Whenever you feel God is impressing something on your heart, journal it out. One of the goals is to be more receptive to how God is speaking in everyday life.

• *Reflect on the moment.* Take time to reflect on what has influenced you. Write down how the moment affected you—what you were thinking and feeling.

- *List a Scripture.* Think of a Scripture verse or passage that corresponds to what God is saying and write it down. Meditate on that Scripture.

- *Write a prayer.* Write out your response to God in a written prayer.

- *Reach out.* Identify a way to reach out to someone else as a result of how God has touched you.

Here is an example of this journaling process. It is my own journal entry from Sunday, October 21, 2001:

Reading the moment: Yesterday was a very affirming day teaching the Perspectives Course in the morning on 2,000 years of missions history and leading the Lower Connecticut Concert of Prayer in the evening. . . . It was exciting to see a sense of history and truth catch the hearts of students in the morning, and to see pastors and lay leaders catch a vision for unity in the evening. David Sue's (Perspectives Course coordinator) words were very affirming. The affirmation of the pastors was very significant from last night as well.

Reflecting on the moment: It is always invigorating to be in a ministry context beyond just the planning and office work side of things. I was encouraged by all of the leadership that is emerging.

Scripture: Genesis 12: the determination of God to bless all people

Prayer: Jesus, help me to affirm others this day as you have affirmed me.

Reaching out: To my son, Jordan—may he grow up into the destiny of his name that all peoples of the earth might know you through him. I will spend one-on-one time with Jordan over bagels on Sunday morning before church doing Scripture study.

In addition to journaling, I spend time meditating on a passage of Scripture. Many people like to read through the Bible every year, and there are many guides to help one accomplish that goal. I often pick a few large sections or books. For example, one year I read through Luke and Acts, which adds up to fifty-two chapters, one chapter for every week of the year. Another year I read carefully and slowly through the book of Isaiah.

There are many devotional guides and prayer guides available in Christian bookstores and through Christian organizations. There are even online devotionals that will pop up every morning when you turn your computer on! The main thing is, spend some time focusing your mind and heart on the Word of God.

After journaling and meditating, I pray a passage of Scripture back to God. Using the pattern that Nehemiah devised (he records it in the first chapter of the book of Nehemiah), I begin with worship, then confession, then I give thanks to God, and finally I intercede for others. A popular acronym to remember the order of this kind of praying is ACTS: adoration, confession, thanksgiving and supplication.

For example, if I read Genesis chapter 12 in my devotional time, my prayer might look like this:

Worship: I would worship the Lord for how he spoke to Abraham, for his determination to bless all the nations of the earth and for his promise to Abraham to make Abraham's name great.

Confession: I would confess any unbelief I've had about God's promises or any failure to exercise the fruits of the Spirit in the past day.

Thanksgiving: I would thank God for bothering to reach down to humanity in the first place, redeeming Abraham and everyone else who would follow the Lord. I would thank God for speaking to me; for working out his purposes in my life; for letting me live in a community where all the nations of the world coexist; for the privilege of teaching and leading in the Perspectives Course and the Lower Connecticut Concert of Prayer.

Intercession: I would pray for the church around the world, the church in Greater New York and my local church; for my family; for the organization I work for; for daily provision. I would bring to the Lord any special needs I know of.

These are just a few ideas about structuring personal devotional time. Speak to older Christians in your church and ask them about their devotional lives and how they spend time with Jesus. Our churches house a wealth of spiritual experience and wisdom, and all we need to do is ask.

THE SECOND DIMENSION: PRAYER IN THE FAMILY

For many people, family prayer is the most difficult prayer rhythm to sustain. Unfortunately, this is especially true of ministry leaders, whose schedules often require them to be away from home during the evening. When children are small and the parents are exhausted, it is best to keep family prayer times short. With older children, try to include them in the worship rather than making them be spectators.

The hardest part of having a family prayer time is often simply finding a time slot that's open in the hectic schedules of all the family members. Many jobs require irregular hours, and in many families both parents work outside the home or a single parent is juggling all the tasks of the household.

The other dynamic that hinders family prayer is that it requires a level of disclosure that many are uncomfortable with. Most adults today are on overload! There is too much to do and too little margin in the day to relax and reflect. A sense of overload is created when people are rushing from task to task, from appointment to appointment, feeling "stressed out," perhaps having stress-related emotional or even physical pain. Disclosure takes time and consistency, both of which are lacking in most of our lives.

My family has discovered that family prayer is often best accomplished when attempted at the beginning of the week. Sunday or Monday evening, we gather after dinner for a time of family devotions. As my children are now teens and preteens, we take turns reading a Scripture passage or praying through a missionary letter.

A while back, as Marya and I talked about our values and prayed together, we came up with a "family mission statement" that consisted of four family values we hold dear. We shared them with our children and brainstormed together about our family life and what God was calling us to as a family. As you work on a family mission statement you will get a clearer sense of what God is calling you to as a family and how to direct your family prayers. Here is our statement:

1. Our family is committed to sacred relationships. This includes our marriage, our children, our friends, our brothers and sisters in Christ and our coworkers. We are committed to praying for each of these important and sacred relationships.

2. We are committed to using our home as a refuge for others. During one year Marya and I welcomed over fifty guests into our home overnight and fed about three hundred guests a home-cooked meal. During our twenty-one years of marriage we have had four young women live with us for extended periods of time—a Hungarian woman and her son, a Trinidadian college student, a young Guyanese woman from our church and a young woman who was being discipled in another local church. As people pass through our home, be it for a night or a year, they become a temporary part of our family and are included in our prayer life. The children help to fulfill this value as well when they spend time talking with guests or give up their bed for a night.

3. *We are committed to reaching out to people in our neighborhood and at work.* Marya has developed strong relationships with the patients, nurses and doctors she works with. When we first moved into our current home we befriended a little Colombian girl who lived next door to us.

4. *We are committed to work toward revival in our region.* As a family we pray for my work with pastors and leaders, and we pray for revival in our region. We pray for our children and the other young people at the local church youth group. Our oldest daughter, Anna, led the first "See You at the Pole" effort at her Catholic high school in Queens.

THE THIRD DIMENSION:
PRAYER IN THE LOCAL CHURCH

At 5:30 a.m., when most people are still sleeping, as many as five hundred people are gathered at the Korean Church of Queens. I visited the early morning prayer meeting at this Korean church with a former staff member, David Sue, in the spring of 1996. The service, held in Korean, begins with singing. The pastor then delivers a short meditation. At least half of the time is spent in simultaneous, crying-out-loud-to-the-Lord prayer. The passion and desperation for God are almost palpable. They have learned the four prerequisites of powerful prayer. They pray in desperation and in unity; it is sustained; their praying is inspired by the Spirit.

As difficult as most of us find it to miss a meal, that's just how difficult it should be to miss our prayer time.

Early morning prayer is not limited to the Korean church. Many churches, like Van Nest Assembly of God in the Bronx, have held early morning prayer meetings for years. Scattered throughout the region and the country are churches faithfully participating in daily morning prayer.

Likewise, twenty-four-hour prayer in the church is not limited to Uganda. Bay Ridge Christian Center in Brooklyn never closes its doors; there is always at least one person in the church praying. A movement called The House of David has recently begun twenty-four-hour prayer in churches in the New York/New Jersey region.

High-profile churches such as Times Square Church and Brooklyn Tabernacle have powerful—and packed—weekly prayer meetings. It has been said that attendance at Sunday morning worship demonstrates the popularity of the preacher, but attendance at Wednesday night prayer meeting demonstrates the popularity of God. This is a sad statement for many of our churches that are largely empty during midweek prayer meetings. But praise God for the growing number of churches that are filling up at midweek for prayer.

At the Tuesday night prayer meeting at Brooklyn Tabernacle, people start lining up to get into the church an hour before the 7:00 p.m. prayer begins. Every Tuesday night it is standing room only in the church—for a prayer meeting! Early in his ministry, Pastor Jim Cymbala realized how important prayer is for the local church, and he made the weekly prayer meeting a priority. One of the elements that makes the prayer meeting at Brooklyn Tabernacle so vibrant is that all the church leaders attend, including the pastors. Pastor Cymbala tells his members, "If you have to choose between missing Sunday morning worship or missing Tuesday night prayer, come to the prayer meeting."

One of the most crucial elements in an effective local church prayer meeting is the presence of the senior pastor. The church has a spiritual authority structure, and what the senior pastor models is far more important than what he preaches.

Another important element in effective church prayer meetings is vibrant worship. Music is one good way to focus on the Lord.

Whether you use a pianist, guitar player, worship band or just a strong voice to lead out in song, worship adds an important dimension to the local prayer meeting.

Variety is also important in an effective prayer meeting. You may want to vary the format from week to week. Pray as a large group sometimes; other times break up into small groups; allow time for individual prayer as well. Try conversational prayer, with each person adding a comment on the same topic as the previous person, just like a regular conversation. There's nothing that kills people's enthusiasm for the prayer meeting more quickly than listening to one or two of the saints give long-winded speeches that cover the whole planet and beyond. Be creative in helping your people pray.

THE FOURTH DIMENSION: COMMUNITYWIDE PRAYER

Every Tuesday morning, from a dozen to twenty pastors gather at a local church in Flushing to share and pray together. This pastors' prayer group has been meeting, in one form or another, for about twelve years. The pastors in the group come from various denominations: Baptist, Presbyterian, charismatic, Assemblies of God. And they come from diverse ethnic backgrounds: Chinese, Korean, Hispanic, European. This little group of pastors is committed to each other. They encourage one another in their respective ministries, and they pray together. They pray not only for each other but for the community they live and minister in and for the whole of New York City as well.

The level of community that has been established over the years is a beautiful picture of unity in diversity. Camaraderie and joyful fellowship mark their meetings. They preach in one another's pulpits; they hold joint services together on Easter; they hold joint baptismal services. One Sunday night twenty-eight people were baptized from their respective churches.

Faithfully facilitating the group is Rev. Conrad Sauer. He is a co-pastor at Immanuel Community Church and also ministers with Here's Life Greater New York. Conrad calls each pastor every Monday evening to remind them of the Tuesday gathering. Having worked with pastors for more than twenty years, Conrad knows how easily distracted and discouraged pastors can be, and he has a ministry of encouragement to them.

What is the secret of their longevity and success? They have covenanted to meet together and care for one another. These pastors know that love is spelled T-I-M-E. We can only love that which we know. We will only know others as we spend time with them.

In lower Connecticut, twenty to twenty-five pastors meet quarterly to pray together. Lay ministry leaders meet monthly at a local church and act as a steering committee for the Lower Connecticut Concerts of Prayer. The united prayer movement in Connecticut is fairly new; they have only been uniting in regionwide prayer for the last two years. As they meet, the desire for unity grows, so they begin to meet more frequently and plan for more unified prayer efforts.

THE FIFTH DIMENSION: CITYWIDE AND NATIONWIDE PRAYER

In Metro New York pastors gather every year for three days of prayer and fellowship at the Pastors' Prayer Summit. Concerts of Prayer Greater New York has coordinated this yearly gathering since 1991, and at the 2002 Summit almost 300 pastors came together in united prayer. Other areas of the country, most notably Oregon, also host annual prayer gatherings for pastors.

One opportunity for citywide prayer for the whole church is the National Day of Prayer. The history behind the National Day of Prayer goes back to the formation of the United States. In 1775 Congress called the colonies to set aside a day for prayer; and in 1863 President Lincoln called for a national day of "humiliation, fasting and prayer." In 1952 President Truman signed into law the National Day of Prayer, and in 1988 President Reagan signed a bill designating the first Thursday of May as the date to celebrate the National Day of Prayer. Today, many church folk across the country observe the National Day of Prayer by gathering in local churches or large arenas to pray for their own cities and the nation. The nationally broadcast concert of prayer can be viewed via satellite in the United States, Canada and Latin America, and on the Internet worldwide.

Opportunities for nationwide prayer are somewhat limited, but when nationwide gatherings are called, by all means try to attend and participate. Promise Keepers holds rallies in cities, but it has also held nationwide gatherings. The Call NYC, held June 29, 2002, invited people from across the country to pray and fast for New York City and the nation. These prayer gatherings, sometimes called "solemn assemblies," offer a glimpse of God bringing our nation together in his name to accomplish his purposes on earth.

Prayer begins in the heart, in the home, but extends to cities, to nations, to the world. God begins a work in one person who can ultimately affect the destiny of a nation. In chapters nine and ten you will find specific ideas and instructions for facilitating a citywide prayer movement in your town or city. Whether you live in Jackson, Mississippi, or Avon, South Dakota, in San Diego, California, or Philadelphia, Pennsylvania, God will move in your city in response to your prayers. Indeed, if God can work in Metro New York City, surely he can transform your city as well!

QUESTIONS FOR REFLECTION OR DISCUSSION

1. What prerequisite for prayer needs the most attention in your life?
2. What rhythm of prayer needs the most attention in your life (personal, family, church, city, nation)?
3. What resource do you need to encourage your prayer life (a book, a study guide, visiting the prayer meeting of another church)?

Next step: Identify a prayer partner with whom you can share your ideas for growing your prayer life, then hold each other accountable weekly.

4

TRANSFORMING PRAYER
FOR A BROKEN CITY

Never underestimate the power of a praying woman. And especially, never underestimate the power of a praying mother.

Richard Galloway had a praying mother. She raised him in a Christian home and regularly prayed for him. When Richard got married, bought a house and drifted away from the church, his mother prayed that God would "put someone on site" to pray for her son. God answered her prayer by providing a live-in housekeeper who knew and loved the Lord Jesus Christ. Richard's housekeeper prayed for him daily as she witnessed his descent into a life of drug and alcohol abuse. With two women praying for him daily, it's no surprise that God revealed himself to Richard in a powerful way.

At the close of the seventies, Richard and Dixie Galloway were quite successful by the world's standards. They had originally purchased a few convenience stores, and they ended up owning a bank, real estate, three corporations and four partnerships—with a net worth of over one million dollars. They had arrived; they were living "the good life." Or were they?

Richard's wife, Dixie, wasn't satisfied with "the good life." When her aunt died she was propelled into a spiritual crisis. Dixie accepted Christ. Then she promptly confronted Richard: "You've tried everything else, why don't you try God?"

It was true. He had tried success and wealth, drugs and booze, parties and popularity. But he was unfulfilled—he was empty inside.

When challenged by his wife to "try God," Richard got down on his knees and prayed a simple prayer: "Help me, Lord." As he prayed, Richard had a profound understanding that he was not alone anymore.

After kneeling before God, Richard read the Bible for three days and nights, with little sleep or food and no drugs or alcohol. He describes the experience of coming to know Christ and changing his lifestyle as "getting out of jail." The pornographic magazines, alcohol and cigarettes came off the shelves of his stores. Later he sold everything and moved to the Caribbean. After three years of living in the Caribbean and leading over 270 young people to Christ, Richard moved to Dallas. It was there, at a Bible study with five men, that God used Isaiah 58 to further change his life. Richard experienced the transforming power of prayer.

New York City has also experienced the transforming power of prayer. The latest upsurge of prayer has taken place in the last decade.

THE FOUR R'S

When the prayer movement in New York City was in its early stages, in the spring of 1994, a group of Christian business leaders, pastors and ministry leaders gathered in a midtown Manhattan hotel to pray for revival. We asked the question, "What would it look like if God were to actually visit New York?"

Out of that meeting four themes emerged. We concluded that God was committed to

- revival
- reconciliation
- reformation
- reaching the lost

Our prayers would be directed to these four areas as we prayed for the transformation of our city. A covenant was drafted and has led our prayers for transformation of the city for the past eight years:

Metro New York Covenant for Prayer and Revival

With repentance and hope, as leaders in Christ's church in Metro New York City, we covenant to unite in prayer to seek God for revival in the church, reconciliation among the churches and races, reformation in society, and reaching the lost. We call others to join in praying with us until God answers, and will take action as He does.

The church needed revival. According to a poll taken by *Christianity Today*, the average pastor prayed a measly seven minutes a day in the late seventies, and it was not much better in the mid-nineties. Many of our churches were prayerless and powerless.

The church needed reconciliation. The unity Christ spoke of in John 17 was largely nonexistent. The church was divided across racial, denominational and geographic lines. We wanted to reflect the church as Jesus sees it—not as Asian, African, Latino, European, not as Presbyterian, Pentecostal, Baptist, Lutheran, Catholic. Jesus sees the beautiful bride of Christ. So we have been praying to that end: that God would unite the bride of Christ and break down the walls that divide us.

The church and society needed reformation. In 1994 the number of murders in New York City was 1,582. In most other large cities in America, also, crime was rampant. The disparity between the rich and the poor was wide and growing wider. The median income for a family in midtown Manhattan was approximately $300,000, while just two miles north, in Harlem, the median income was a paltry $10,000. We believed that God wanted to transform the seven cultural pillars of our society: education, government, medicine, business, community, media and religion.

The church needed to share the gospel. We recognized that although myriad needs existed in our city, people's ultimate need is spiritual. Twenty million people live within seventy-five miles of Times Square. That's one out of every 300 people in the world! New York is the largest Jewish city in the world, with more Jews than Jerusalem. New York City has the largest immigrant neighborhood: Chinatown. And there are more Puerto Ricans in New York than in Puerto Rico. The world is at our doorstep . . . no, it's in our living room! And the world needs Jesus.

REVIVAL: GIVING GOD NO REST

In 1727 Nicholas Count von Zinzendorf was leading a group of Christian refugees on his estate in Moravia, Germany. Zinzendorf welcomed these refugees who had fled from religious persecution. He discipled them and imparted a vision

> *"We are trying to make our communities another Nazareth, where Jesus can come and rest awhile."*
>
> MOTHER TERESA,
> *WORDS TO LOVE BY*

for revival and missions. As different denominations joined the burgeoning religious community, divisions arose. Zinzendorf called the believers together for worship and Communion, to seek God together and ask God to heal the divisions among them.

As they took Communion together, the Holy Spirit visited them in a powerful way, and the members were convicted of their divisive spirit. Church historians have labeled this event the "Moravian Pentecost." As the 400 refugees wept and embraced one another, they experienced unity and healing. This Communion service launched the beginning of a daily prayer vigil that was to span the next one hundred years. Yes, a one-hundred-year prayer meeting: *Hernhut* in German, or the Lord's Watch.

Church historian Richard Lovelace has described the Lord's Watch as the most vibrant expression of Christianity since the early church.

This first Lord's Watch rested on the promise of Isaiah 62:6-7:

I have posted watchmen on your walls, O Jerusalem;
    they will never be silent day or night.
You who call on the LORD,
    give yourselves no rest,
and give him no rest till he establishes Jerusalem
    and makes her the praise of the earth.

They began with 24 people who faithfully spent one hour in intercession every day. During the years that followed, more than 300 missionaries were raised up from that community. In fact, it was in a prayer group in London, led by a Moravian missionary, that John and Charles Wesley made their commitments to Jesus Christ. John Wesley then traveled to the Zinzendorf estate for a time of discipleship by the Moravians before he launched his preaching ministry that changed the face of the church.

On February 1, 1995, we began our own Lord's Watch in Metro New York City. It is a modernized, urbanized edition of what the Moravians envisioned for their day. The Lord's Watch is described in detail in chapter nine. Through it God has already raised up scores of churches and thousands of individual believers who have covenanted together to cover one day a month with intercessory prayer.

The promises of Isaiah 62:6-7 are still true for us today. We have been praying for God to unleash a "river of prayer" that will impact not only our region but the whole earth. With the truly international makeup of the New York area, a genuine spiritual awakening in our city has the potential to impact every corner of the earth for Christ.

And God has answered in powerful ways. Here are just a few examples:

1. Unity in the body of Christ: Women's Prayer Summit (3,000 women two years consecutively); Promise Keepers (35,000 men at Shea Stadium); National Day of Prayer (up to 6,000 gathered at churches across the metro area).

2. The restraint of evil: violent crime decreased by 70 percent between 1995 and 2000; protection of tens of thousands of people on 9/11.

3. Coalition building: emergence of cooperative networks in the aftermath of 9/11, unifying to serve the body of Christ—Network NYC Coalition; Northeast Clergy Group.

4. Collaborative community development: rebuilding $200 million in housing in the Harlem area; thousands of homes built in the Bronx and Brooklyn through the Nehemiah project; development of the Leadership Academy and other charter schools.

5. International events: Good Friday peace accord in Northern Ireland; 900 church planters raised up in Bihar, North India.

RECONCILIATION: A PLACE FOR ALL GOD'S PEOPLE (ISAIAH 56)

Rev. Russell Rosser came to Flushing, Queens, in 1978 and became the pastor of First Baptist Church of Flushing. The neighborhood was undergoing great changes. At the start of the eighties, Flushing was 10 percent Asian. By 1990 Flushing was 50 percent Asian as immigrants from Hong Kong and Seoul poured in. As Pastor Rosser drove to church, he would often pass a Jewish synagogue just a few blocks away, and he would see the inscription above the doorpost: "For my house will be called a house of prayer for all nations." Pastor Rosser saw the unique opportunity to translate that doorpost inscription (taken from Is 56:7) into a living congregational reality.

During the twenty-two years of his pastorate, the church developed three vibrant congregations: English, Spanish and Chinese. There was great diversity even within the congregations. The English congregation was composed of African Americans, West Indians, Asians, East Indians, Latinos, Europeans and others. The Spanish congregation had immigrants from many Central and South American countries. And the Chinese congregation was primarily Hong Kong immigrants, with many Taiwanese immigrants as well. The church thrived as it lived out its mission to take the Word of God to the world of God. First Baptist Church is a picture of unity in diversity.

Isaiah 56 is the intermediate fulfillment of God's promise in Genesis 12 to bless all the nations of the earth. It is the preview of the portrait in Revelation 5 of an international prayer meeting attended by believers from every tribe and tongue, along with 100 million angels. God's house is a house of prayer for all the nations, and we continue to pray for the fulfillment of Isaiah 56 in our day.

Many churches in New York are monocultural, some due to language barriers and others by choice. But more and more churches are international. And even those churches that are monocultural and monoracial are joining with other churches in united prayer in unprecedented numbers. As pastors' prayer groups form in neighborhoods across the city, they experience the joy of fellowship with believers from other traditions and other races. Pastors return to their congregations and encourage their members to attend National Day of Prayer gatherings in regional churches so that they too can experience unity and reconciliation as they pray with believers from other cultures, races and denominations. Once you have experienced united prayer and get a taste for "a house of prayer for all nations," you will be spoiled for anything less!

REFORMATION: TRUE FASTING (ISAIAH 58)

When Richard Galloway read Isaiah 58, his life changed. It was that dramatic. He felt God saying to him, "If you really want to know what I care about, read this." Richard saw not only the commands but the promises. To him it was a no-brainer. Do what God has commanded, feed the poor, provide housing for the homeless, provide clothes for the naked—and *God will bless us.*

> "Is not this the kind of fasting I have chosen:
> to loose the chains of injustice
>   and untie the cords of the yoke,
> to set the oppressed free
>   and break every yoke?
> Is it not to share your food with the hungry
>   and to provide the poor wanderer with shelter—
> when you see the naked, to clothe him,
>   and not to turn away from your own flesh and blood?
> Then your light will break forth like the dawn,
>   and your healing will quickly appear;
> then your righteousness will go before you,
>   and the glory of the LORD will be your rear guard.
> Then you will call, and the LORD will answer;
>   you will cry for help, and he will say: Here am I
> "If you do away with the yoke of oppression,
>   with the pointing finger and malicious talk,
> and if you spend yourselves in behalf of the hungry
>   and satisfy the needs of the oppressed,
> then your light will rise in the darkness,
>   and your night will become like the noonday." (Is 58:6-10)

Richard was led to Stony Brook School on Long Island. They told him, "We have an old school bus we don't need, and we want to help the homeless in New York City." Richard and his wife, Dixie, started to pray. They felt called to work among the poor, but they had no resources or experience. Richard thought either God was up to something or they had lost their minds. God was up to something.

As they prayed, God showed them how to use the bus to serve the homeless in New York City. And as they prayed, God began to provide for their financial needs. One Tuesday, Richard received a $5 donation. God revealed to him that this small gift was a seed—there was more to come. Sure enough, the next day a $50 donation came in. On Thursday a woman donated $500 to the fledgling ministry. And on Friday a $5,000 check came in. Richard and Dixie were very grateful but by this time not very surprised!

This was the inauspicious beginning of New York City Relief. Since 1989 this ministry to the poor of New York City has reached literally thousands of people, providing soup, prayer, referral to drug treatment and shelters, and myriad other resources. But Richard is careful to point out that their product is not soup but hope. They make connections and bring the presence of God to the streets. Over the years Richard has learned that by serving the poor, one is serving Jesus Christ. Something Mother Teresa once said resonated strongly with Richard. Her modus operandi was, "Pray four hours a day, then go out and look for Jesus in disguise."

John Clause also works among the poor in New York City. John was trained as a lawyer and became CEO of a real estate development company in the 1980s. Like Richard Galloway, he was financially successful but spiritually bankrupt. When the bottom fell out of the real estate market, he became personally and professionally bankrupt as well and had to file for chapter 7. Although he had grown up in a Christian home, his faith was practically nonexistent by this time.

When he met his future wife, Susan, she insisted that he go to church with her at Smithtown Gospel Tabernacle. At the first service John attended, at the first altar call he heard, he went forward and accepted Jesus Christ as his personal Savior.

John knew what it was to be rich, and he knew what it felt like to be poor. After becoming a Christian, he felt called to work with the poor. Isaiah 58 played a pivotal role in his life, and he longed to be a catalyst in "loosing the chains of injustice." His calling and the mission of World Vision were in close alignment.

World Vision is an international partnership of Christians whose mission is to follow our Lord and Savior Jesus Christ in working with the poor and oppressed to promote human transformation, seek justice and bear witness to the good news of the kingdom of God.

John accepted a position with World Vision. He was preparing for the launch of the New York City office of World Vision in September 2001, when 9/11 hit.

The World Vision New York staff team of fourteen prayed for direction that day. They wanted to provide support to the victims, and they knew "our best partner would be the church." The American Families Assistance Fund was set up, and almost $6 million was donated to help relieve the financial burden of those who lost family members or jobs at the World Trade Center. Instead of simply mailing checks to approved applicants, World Vision decided to personally hand out the checks to people, using local churches as the meeting place. Over 2,300 individuals have received financial assistance—along with prayer and a kind word as they went to the church to pick up their check.

One recipient was an Ecuadorian man who was wounded and lost his job at the World Trade Center. His wife was present when he received his check. She told the World Vision representative, "Forty-one years ago you sponsored me as a child in Ecuador." Now, forty-one years later, World Vision ministered to her and her husband by providing for them in their time of emergency need.

Isaiah tells us that when we care for the poor our light will shine out like the dawn. Thank God for the lights shining out of New York City—lights like Richard Galloway and John Clause. The transformation of New York, or any city, will take place only as God's people respond to his call to minister to the poor.

REACHING THE LOST: GOOD NEWS (ISAIAH 61)

Raymond Rivera grew up in a Roman Catholic family in East Harlem. *West Side Story* wasn't just a movie or a play—it was the reality of his boyhood. He was prohibited from venturing east of Third Avenue; that was Italian territory. When he was fourteen his family moved to Brownsville, Brooklyn, and Ray became a minority—the only Latino in an Italian neighborhood. As he learned to make friends in an unfamiliar and often painful context, Ray was being prepared for a lifelong ministry of racial reconciliation.

At an evangelistic crusade in Brooklyn, Ray gave his life to Christ. Here is the story, in his own words:

> The evangelists would pray for the sick, and my friends and I made out that we were healed. Everyone in the tent was praising God, and we were laughing at them. But something kept drawing us back. The evangelists rented the place for three weeks, and we went back every night. The last night of the campaign, the evangelists invited us to a deteriorated storefront Pentecostal church in Brownsville that held fifty people—when it rained outside it rained inside. It was there that I accepted Christ as my personal Savior.[1]

After Ray graduated from New York Theological Seminary he was called to pastor Melrose Reformed Church in the South Bronx. In the following years Ray rose through the hierarchy of the Reformed Church in America and eventually became National Secretary for Hispanic Ministries. His passion, his driving force, was to integrate his faith with his desire for justice. Ray's ministry could be summed up by the first verse of Isaiah 61. Isaiah 61:1 combines justice and evangelism in a poignant calling:

> The Spirit of the Sovereign LORD is on me,
>> because the LORD has anointed me
>> to preach good news to the poor.
> He has sent me to bind up the brokenhearted,
>> to proclaim freedom for the captives
>> and release from darkness for the prisoners.

Isaiah 61 was an important Old Testament passage for Jesus. As he began his public ministry in Luke 4, Jesus quoted from Isaiah 61. He saw his earthly ministry as one of transformation: preaching good news, healing the brokenhearted and proclaiming freedom. And everywhere Jesus went, lives were changed.

Lives have also been transformed in one of the poorest areas in the United States, the South Bronx. Ray Rivera began a ministry there in 1993. With passion and a proposal, Ray approached the Pew Charitable Trusts and the Aaron Diamond Foundation. His plan outlined a new ministry for Latino churches that combined evangelism and social concern. The Latino Pastoral Action Center (LPAC) was started with two staff members.

Today, LPAC is housed in a $5 million building with a staff of forty and an annual budget of almost $1 million. Ray wants "to lift this building up as a model of what can be done. We want to be a signpost for the twenty-first century that holistic ministry can be done. This is my best effort to present a model that addresses the historical dichotomy in the evangelical church."[2] Ray wants to reach out with the gospel *and* loose the chains of the oppressed. He was led by God to form LPAC "to challenge churches that are Christ-centered to develop a passion for social justice, and liberal churches to develop a passion for evangelism."[3]

Ministries at LPAC include an after-school program; the Family Life Academy (a public alternative elementary school); training for urban ministry programs; community development ministries, including housing projects; and mercy ministries, including an AIDS/HIV ministry. The workers share Christ as they minister to all the needs in the urban family in the twenty-first century. LPAC is an embodiment of Isaiah 61, bringing good news to the poor.

"Believe me when I say that ten Holy-Spirit-led men or women can pressure and even transform huge cities. It's happening everywhere. There is a relationship always between the presence of the godly and the preservation of urban communities."

RAY BAKKE, *A THEOLOGY AS BIG AS THE CITY*

NOT THE SAME CITY

New York City is not the same city in 2002 as it was in 1995. As prayers have gone up, God has answered. Hope is the fruit of our praying. Isaiah fills us with tremendous hope as we see glimpses of what a transformed city can look like.

What fills the horizon of your praying? What is your church praying for? Cities are changed through prayer. We are witnesses to what God can do. Indeed, if God can work in New York City, he can surely work in your city.

The climax of Isaiah's vision for a "city of God" is in Revelation. A portrait is drawn there of a completely transformed city where there is no weeping, no homelessness, no hunger, no despair, no night. All the nations are worshiping before the throne of Christ. Until that time when we are all united in the heavenly city, we will keep praying for God to transform our cities. He can, and he will.

QUESTIONS FOR REFLECTION OR DISCUSSION

1. Can you identify the four R's that churches in Greater New York are praying for?
2. What was one of the answers to prayer from the Lord's Watch over a seven-year period?
3. In Isaiah 61, to whom did Jesus say he came to bring good news?

Next Step: Identify a ministry in your community that is reaching out to the poor and begin praying for them. Meet the director, and offer any assistance you can.

PART TWO

The
BIBLE
and the
CITY

5

RAISING UP A PRAYER LEADER
Hannah and Samuel

Roderick Caesar Sr. immigrated to New York City from the Caribbean island of St. Lucia in 1919. As a merchant marine he sailed around the world delivering goods and supplies to soldiers during WWI. Returning to the streets of Harlem after the war, he was lounging on a street corner when a woman preacher caught his eye and his ear. As he listened more closely, he felt, for the first time in his life, the pull of the Holy Spirit, and right there on that street corner Roderick Caesar Sr. gave his life to Jesus.

The woman preacher took the young Roderick back to her church, Harlem Pentecostal Assembly, and over the next several years Roderick was nurtured and discipled in the faith. His love for God and God's Word grew year by year. He supported himself by driving a taxi and working in maintenance on the subways. In 1928, when God called him to form a church in Queens, he started with a few Bible study and prayer groups in private homes. Bethel Gospel Tabernacle was incorporated as a church on August 22, 1932.

During the past seventy years the church has grown dramatically, planting many other churches both in the United States and abroad, and beginning Bible institutes in Africa, the West Indies and India. Truly, the scope and impact of the ministry of Bethel Gospel Tabernacle is worldwide. What was one of the primary factors for the success and growth of the church? The faithfulness of one woman . . . one praying woman.

Mildred Williams, a longstanding member of Bethel Gospel Tabernacle, approached Roderick Caesar Sr., then Bishop Caesar, in 1973 and told him she felt God leading her to begin an early morning prayer meeting. Her desire was to pray at the church, seven days a week, 365 days a year, at 6:00 a.m. for one hour. Sister Williams showed up at the church faithfully, day after day, even when she was the only one there. The prayer meeting grew over the years and is now one of the hallmarks of the church, an integral part of the life of the church and one of the greatest factors leading to the successful ministry of Bethel. Never underestimate the power of a woman at prayer!

THE MAKING OF A LEADER: 1 SAMUEL 1

Like Sister Williams, Hannah was a praying woman. At the beginning of 1 Samuel, Hannah was in the midst of a personal crisis, even as the nation of Israel itself was in a national crisis. The Philistines had ruled over Israel for twenty years, and the spiritual priesthood of the church was corrupt. Samuel laments in 1 Samuel 3:1, "In those days the word of the LORD was rare; there were not many visions." The nation hit rock bottom in the tenth century B.C. when a Levite appeased the wicked men of Gibeah by sending them his concubine. She was brutally raped and murdered by the evil Israelites. Then her master dismembered her body and sent the twelve body parts into the twelve tribes of Israel (see Judg 19). The nation was amoral and ungodly; the fear of God was nonexistent.

Hannah is introduced into this scene of national turmoil and impending war with one very serious problem: she was barren. Most of us probably know women who have struggled to bear children, and it is heartbreaking. However, while many receive the support of family and friends and the counsel of doctors, Hannah was ostracized by society and ridiculed by her husband's other wife, Peninnah, who had borne children. Barrenness was a disgrace, especially in Jewish culture. Hannah was desperate, and in her desperation she knelt before God in prayer.

Hannah knew that her husband could father children, so the fault must be hers. It is hard to imagine the depth of the grief and longing she must have felt. When her husband, Elkanah, asked, "Don't I mean more to you than ten sons?" (1 Sam 1:8), it is clear that even he did not understand the depth of her grief. In her anguish Hannah wept and prayed before God. Honesty is the language of our praying—we will never learn how to pray until we learn how to weep.

Bishop Roderick Caesar Jr. has learned how to pray, and he has learned how to weep. He followed in his father's footsteps and was installed as the pastor of Bethel Gospel Tabernacle in 1984. Just five years later, his son, Roderick Caesar III, was born three months premature. The doctors did not give Bishop Caesar and his wife, Beverly, any hope to cling to. They were bluntly told their son would die.

They wept and they prayed. They clung to each other and clung to God. Bishop Caesar told me, "When the doctor said 'no way,' God told me, 'I am the way.' " The church united in focused prayer for the tiny infant son. Roderick III lay in the hospital bed for four and a half months, and the church prayed continually for his healing and growth. Keep in mind, twelve years ago the practice of medicine was not as advanced as it is today, and many premature babies did not survive. Praise God that just as he heard Hannah's prayers, he heard the prayers of Bishop Caesar and his wife and all the saints at Bethel. Roderick is now a healthy, happy twelve-year-old boy.

Hannah's crisis was personal, but it was also spiritual. She was confronted with the crisis of unanswered prayer. It hadn't been just a few weeks or months. Hannah had been crying out to God for years: "This went on year after year" (1 Sam 1:7). Meanwhile, her rival, Elkanah's other wife, kept provoking her. Yet she never gave up hope. Hannah continued to call out to God, asking him to bless her with a son.

There are few things more spiritually painful than unanswered prayer. We pray for years about a wayward child or an unconverted loved one—and don't get the answer we so desperately crave. How do we understand the ways of God in these circumstances?

Bishop Roderick Caesar Jr. can think of one painful period in his life when he felt God didn't answer his prayer— the day his mother died twenty-three years ago. The pain has subsided, but it is still there. His father, while wading through his own grief, helped him see the death of their precious wife and mother with an eternal perspective. Roderick Jr. had a godly mother, a praying mother, a loving mother for thirty-one years of his life. Instead of lamenting the loss, his father encouraged him to remember her life with joy.

"We will never learn how to pray until we learn how to weep."

BISHOP GERALD KAUFMAN

Katie and I can identify. My mom died in 1991, and Katie's dad passed away in 1996. Their lives were much shorter than we would have wanted, and our hearts are still sore. All our questions have not been answered; however, we continue to hope in the God who does answer prayer—and whose purposes are eternal.

ONE WOMAN'S PRAYER CHANGES A NATION

Hannah had crises, both personal and spiritual, but she also had great confidence in God. Year after year Hannah's prayer had not been answered, but she continued to pray to the Lord Almighty. She knew

God had the power to give her a son. Although she didn't understand what God was doing, she continued to pray.

Actually, God was the cause of her trouble! It says in 1 Samuel 1:5, "The LORD had closed her womb." Why would God do that to a devoted woman?

I believe I know why. God was concerned for Hannah, but he was also concerned for the nation of Israel. Hannah prayed in 1 Samuel 1:11, "If you will only look upon your servant's misery and remember me, and not forget your servant but give her a son, then I will give him to the LORD for all the days of his life." If God had not closed her womb, it is not likely that Hannah would have prayed such a desperate prayer. And if she had not prayed that prayer, God would not have had a Samuel to work with to transform the spiritual climate of Israel.

God birthed in Hannah a prayer that would change the destiny of the nation. The essence of Hannah's prayer was that God would *remember* her. She promised the Lord that if he gave her a son, she would give him back to the Lord. Notice that Peninnah did not dedicate any of her many sons to the Lord. Hannah was childless—but if God would provide just one son, she would give him back to God. She was serious in her prayer, and she kept her promise.

After years of prayer, God answered Hannah. In 1 Samuel 1:19 the language of Hannah's prayer is repeated in the answer to her prayer: "the LORD remembered her." Just as God remembered Hannah, she remembered her promise to God. Imagine how difficult it would be to give up a son it took years to conceive. Hannah breast-fed her cherished son, Samuel, and then dutifully gave him over to the Lord's service once he was weaned at the age of three. Hannah did not know whether she would conceive any more children, but she kept her promise and gave her firstborn, her only son, to God. At the heart of her relationship to God was a life of surrender. She learned to surrender as she learned to pray.

THE CALLING OF A LEADER (1 SAMUEL 3)

Fifty-two years after Roderick Caesar Sr. founded Bethel Gospel Tabernacle, the mantle of leadership was passed on to his son, Roderick Caesar Jr.—mentor to disciple, elder to younger, father to son. Roderick Jr. was well prepared to take on a spiritual leadership role, having faithfully served as his father's armor bearer for over twenty years.

Roderick Sr. traveled extensively in the ministry, and wherever he went, his son paved the way. No task was too trivial, no detail too insignificant. Roderick Jr. made hotel reservations, confirmed speaking engagements, booked flight schedules and took minutes at meetings. As he accompanied his father he learned how to deal with people, how to study the Scriptures for himself, how to preach and how to pray. The installation service was a truly joyous occasion as, on November 1, 1984, Roderick Caesar Jr. became the full-time pastor of Bethel Gospel Tabernacle.

The mood surrounding the call of Samuel was starkly different. It was early morning, but it was still dark outside. The lamp in the temple was about to flicker out. Samuel, twelve years old, was lying down in the temple, sleeping near the ark of God. Eli, Samuel's mentor, spiritual father and priest, was also asleep in the temple. Eli was losing his eyesight and depended greatly on Samuel. This was the same Eli who had rebuked Hannah for praying, thinking her drunk; the same Eli who had accepted three-year-old Samuel in the temple; the same Eli whose two sons were corrupt and did not follow the Lord.

Samuel was a young man and "did not yet know the LORD. The word of the LORD had not yet been revealed to him" (1 Sam 3:7). So when he heard a voice calling his name, Samuel naturally assumed Eli was calling him. The first time God called, Samuel answered, "Here I am," and ran to Eli to see what he wanted. But Eli hadn't called him. The Lord had called him. The God of the universe called this twelve-year-old boy by name.

Eli instructed Samuel to go back and lie down. Then God called Samuel again, and again Samuel went in to Eli. He was again told to lie down and go back to sleep. Eli might have been getting annoyed with Samuel for interrupting his sleep.

The third time God called Samuel, Eli finally began to catch on that something supernatural was happening. "Eli realized that the LORD was calling the boy" (1 Sam 3:8). So Eli directed Samuel to respond to the Lord if he was called again.

Once more, for the fourth time, God called Samuel. This time the Lord actually "came and stood there" (v. 10) and called him by name twice: "Samuel! Samuel!" The God of the universe persisted in calling a twelve-year-old boy. He called him by name. The God of creation calls us by name as he calls us to serve him.

Finally Samuel responded. "Speak, for your servant is listening" (v.10). In other words, "I am your slave—tell me what to do. I am your servant, how can I serve you?" The calling is a lofty one, but it is also a lowly one. Those who are called by God into leadership in his church are servants, slaves of the Lord.

God was going to judge Eli, and he told young Samuel his plan. Eli had not restrained his sons; he had not kept them from evil. Maybe he was so busy in the temple that he had not paid attention to his own family. But it was inexcusable. A man of God must keep his own house in order. Eli apparently knew about the sins his sons were engaging in but did not restrain them.

Remember now, Samuel was a mere twelve-year-old boy. He was hearing the voice of God, and the message God gave him was a hard one. Samuel was asked to carry the message of God's judgment to the very man who had taught him much of what he knew about God. The man who had been like a father to him, who had nurtured him and raised him in the temple since he was three years old, was under the judgment of God.

It's no wonder Samuel couldn't sleep that night. As morning dawned, Samuel opened the doors of the temple. He was afraid to tell Eli what God had revealed to him. Eli called Samuel and—perhaps sensing impending judgment—warned Samuel not to hide anything. "Give it to me straight," Eli said in essence. "Don't water it down, and don't leave anything out."

So the first task Samuel was given, as a twelve-year-old emerging leader, was to pronounce the judgment of God on the priest. Samuel had a dreadful choice: to stay silent and protect Eli, risking God's judgment, or to obey God and tell his spiritual father that he and his family would be judged by God. Samuel surrendered to God; he chose to fear God rather than to fear Eli.

Like Samuel, leaders often have difficult choices to make. As leaders follow God they are often misunderstood by the people they lead. But following God is always the best choice.

Samuel's obedience was rewarded with the presence of God. "The LORD was with Samuel as he grew up, and he let none of his words fall to the ground" (1 Sam 3:19). Samuel chose God, and God honored Samuel. At the beginning of chapter 3, "the word of the LORD was rare," but as chapter 4 begins, "Samuel's word came to all Israel." Because of one man's obedience, a nation heard from God. Because one leader chose to follow God and fear God rather than man, the entire nation of

Israel was blessed. Samuel's early life is a testimony to the truth that our spiritual influence is in direct proportion to our intimacy with God.

Although Roderick Caesar Jr. was raised in a Christian home, he did not always follow God. When Roderick Jr. was nineteen years old, God called him. It was not unlike God's call on Samuel, or on you and me. As Roderick describes the experience, he says "the Lord put me up in the corner and said I had few options." Option one: follow me. There was no option two. That was the only option given. God made it clear to Roderick Jr. that he, the living God, would not be in anything that didn't honor him. Roderick Jr. had a choice to make. Like Samuel, like Hannah, he chose to surrender to God.

THE IMPACT OF A LEADER (1 SAMUEL 7)

After God called Samuel, the Philistines defeated the nation of Israel, and the ark of God was stolen. The nation of Israel was in turmoil. When the ark of God was returned, Samuel assumed a prophetic leadership role and called the entire nation of Israel to gather in Mizpah. Samuel had the authority to speak to all of Israel, because God had all of Samuel.

Chapter 7 opens with the dramatic confrontation between Samuel and the nation of Israel. The Israelites have been worshiping Baal and Ashtoreth, the god and goddess of fertility, love and war. They have been indulging in all kinds of sexually immoral practices, and God will not deliver them until they repent and vow to serve him alone.

Samuel is very direct as he addresses the throngs of people gathered before him.

> And Samuel said to the whole house of Israel, "If you are returning to
> the LORD with all your hearts, then rid yourselves of the foreign gods
> and the Ashtoreths and commit yourselves to the LORD and serve him

only, and he will deliver you out of the hand of the Philistines."
(1 Sam 7:3)

Israel responds to Samuel's call for repentance and holiness, and as
a nation they turn back to God with an undivided heart and put away
their false idols. Samuel then leads Israel in a day of confession and
fasting. As Samuel leads in prayer, all the people fast and confess their
sins before God.

In recent years the church in America has been called to nationwide or citywide gatherings of prayer and fasting. Groups such as
Promise Keepers and The Call have gathered hundreds of thousands
of believers for an extended day of prayer, repentance and fasting. First
Samuel provides a model and sets a precedent for these modern-day
assemblies.

As Israel is assembled and Samuel is crying out to God on their
behalf, the Philistines see an opportunity they can't pass up. What a
great chance to attack Israel! There they all are gathered together in
one place. As the Philistines attack, the Israelites begin to panic, but
Samuel continues to pray. Samuel's prayer is their only defense, and
God answers Samuel's prayer.

How did God answer? He thundered. Why is that so significant? It
rarely thunders in Israel. God made himself unmistakably known as
Israel gathered in repentance and prayer. The Israelites defeated the
Philistine army by the grace of God.

There are precious moments in our lives when God arrives on the
scene. There is no other explanation for some events; God's hand is
undeniable. For us, one of these moments was in February 1989.

We were planning our third concert of prayer for Greater New
York. The night before it was to start, weather forecasters predicted a
100 percent chance of a blizzard blanketing New York City. Beginning

to panic (not unlike the Israelites), I called up my coleader, Aida Force, and asked her advice. "Do we need to cancel the event? reschedule it? What should we do?" Aida calmly replied that we should just pray for the snowstorm to go out to sea. I hadn't thought of that!

The next day almost a foot of snow fell on Atlantic City, about sixty miles to our south, on the shores of the Atlantic Ocean. Not one flake of snow fell on New York City. The concert of prayer attracted a large crowd and the presence of God was very powerful.

The next day, Sunday, Aida was standing outside her church when it began to snow lightly. As a snowflake kissed her cheek it mingled with her tears of gratitude for a prayer-answering God.

A LEADER'S LEGACY

After their victory against the Philistines, Samuel took a stone, set it up near Mizpah and named it Ebenezer, which is translated "stone of help" or "thus far has the Lord helped us." Samuel wanted a permanent reminder of God's hand of deliverance. He didn't want the Israelites to forget that when they repented and prayed, God answered them.

Max DePree defines leadership in this way: "The first responsibility of a leader is to define reality. The last is to say thank you. In between the two, the leader must become a servant and a debtor."[1] Building on this, we could say that Samuel demonstrates the three primary callings of a spiritual leader: to define reality, to call people to prayer and to say thank you.

Bishop Caesar Sr. died on June 26, 1999. He was ninety-eight years old. At his funeral, Greater Allen A.M.E. Cathedral of New York was packed with local clergy, parishioners, family members, neighbors and visiting dignitaries. It was an Ebenezer moment as the people remembered the man of God and his ministry with love and respect. His preaching ministry had spanned fifty-two years, and during that time he defined reality, called people to prayer and gave God thanks. The legacy he left behind in his son, daughter and grandchildren will continue for years to come.

The theme verse chosen for Bishop Caesar's funeral was 1 Samuel 2:30: "For them that honor me I will honor" (KJV). Funerals are a time to honor our loved ones who have passed, but funerals are also a time to honor God. At Bishop Caesar's funeral everyone who spoke "remembered God" and testified to the hand of God in Bishop's life. Bishop Ezra Williams, pastor emeritus of Bethel Gospel Assembly in Harlem, said "Bishop Caesar was the instrument God used to launch me into leadership in the ministry."

The Three Primary Callings of a Spiritual Leader
1. Define reality.
2. Call people to prayer.
3. Say thank you.

Most important of all, his five grandchildren honored their grandpa—and honored God—in their dedication: "Grandpa, you will always be in our hearts, and all that you taught us will be indelibly imprinted on our minds. We will make you proud. We will honor your name."

After the funeral, the tombstone, the stone of remembrance, was placed on Bishop Caesar's grave. Like the Ebenezer stone, it serves as a reminder of the goodness of God in one man's life, and a reminder of how one man who is surrendered to God can affect the destiny of many, even a nation.

First Samuel 7 closes with a summary of Samuel's ministry as a judge. He was appointed and equipped by God to keep Israel in a right relationship with God. He traveled to the cities Mizpah, Bethel and Gilgal, but he always returned home to Ramah. At home he established an altar where he would worship, remembering in prayer all that God had done for Israel.

Hannah surrendered Samuel to God when he was three; Samuel surrendered his own life to God at the age of twelve. Just as God used Samuel to change the destructive path Israel was on, to lead Israel into the paths of righteousness, God still uses people today who surrender to him, to impact nations.

God is still looking for people of prayer who will surrender to him. He is still seeking leaders who will follow him at any cost. The call to leadership is not an easy one; it is costly. But there is no higher calling than to be a servant of God.

We can learn a lot from Hannah and Samuel. God can use the praying of one broken person to change the destiny of a nation or a city—your nation, your city. God has used Bishops Roderick Caesar Sr. and Jr. over the past seventy years to impact not only New York City but also many other parts of the world.

God will use the spiritual authority and authenticity of a leader to call a city or a nation to prayer, purity and transformation. God is raising up young men and women today to lead the church in the twenty-first century. The power of a praying city lies in the brokenness of a praying leader. Is God calling you?

QUESTIONS FOR REFLECTION OR DISCUSSION

1. What two kinds of crises was Hannah experiencing?
2. How did God answer Hannah's personal need and Israel's need all at once?
3. What were the primary qualities of Samuel's life?

Next step: Identify an important leader in your life (family member, pastor, employer, educator, government official). Make a commitment to pray for that person weekly, and tell him or her that you are doing so.

6

REBUILDING AFTER DISASTER
Nehemiah

When asked the question, "What do you want to be when you grow up?" no young person responds, "I want to be a drug addict." Likewise, one will not likely hear a Jewish boy aspire to be a Christian pastor. Jerry Kaufman did not set either of these goals in his youth, but by the grace and mystery of God he became a pastor who was also a recovered addict.

GOD OF THE BROKEN

Gerald Kaufman was raised in a nice Jewish home in the Bronx, but he ended up joining the throngs of young men and women who were sucked under by heroin addiction in the 1960s. His addiction led to criminal behavior, which led to his incarceration. Six times Jerry was sent to prison for drug possession and related crimes. He was on the fast track to nowhere.

Mama Leo was a Puerto Rican evangelist who looked more like an Irish nun, with flaming red hair and bright green eyes. In her limited English she prayed for Jerry Kaufman and led him to Christ. He was healed instantaneously of his addiction. Kaufman attended Zion Bible Institute, and after proving he was serious in his faith commitment and showing himself to be responsible, he was given the ministry of starting an English-speaking youth group. The youth group evolved into a church plant: Love Gospel Assembly. God used this Jewish boy from the Bronx to lead a large black and Hispanic church. Yes, God uses unexpected vessels to accomplish his purposes.

Jerry Kaufman knew what it was to be homeless, to be an addict and to be poor. He wanted any church he was a part of to minister to the real needs of people in the Bronx—the poor, the homeless, the addicted, the hopeless. During the 1970s and 1980s the Bronx began to resemble a war zone as whole city blocks were occupied with burned-out and abandoned buildings. Kaufman felt called by God to stay in the Bronx and to make his church a church for the poor. Since 1980, Love Gospel Assembly has fed hungry people more than two million meals through its daily feeding programs. The church has seventy-five ministries, ranging from healthcare services to immigration outreaches and prayer ministries.

The Jewish boy from the Bronx grew up to become Bishop Gerald Kaufman. His commitment to the Bronx was unflagging, and he required all the staff of Love Gospel to live in the Bronx. Bishop Kaufman died in 1997 and was succeeded by Pastor Ronald L. Bailey, an African American.

A CALL TO NEHEMIAH PRAYING

In March 1992, Bishop Kaufman spoke at our Bronx Pastors' Concert of Prayer. He led a meditation on Nehemiah 1:1-11 and outlined the four conditions of meaningful prayer. (The main points are from Bishop Kaufman, heard by Mac; the reflections are ours.)

---

1. YOU WILL NEVER LEARN TO PRAY
UNTIL YOU ARE CONCERNED ENOUGH TO ASK.

Meet Nehemiah. He was a man living the good life. He had a good job, with great benefits and a generous retirement plan. It was

November, and he was carrying out his daily duties of waiting on the king and tasting the wine before it was offered to the royal palate. One could describe him as a secret service agent B.C. Nehemiah lived in the winter resort of kings, Shushan, Persia. His hometown, Jerusalem, was 750 miles away. King Artaxerxes had picked Nehemiah out and rewarded him for his integrity and honesty. Only someone the king trusted thoroughly would be given the job of cupbearer and guard to the king's sleeping quarters. But though he had a comfortable life, Nehemiah had moments of homesickness, and thoughts of his home were never far away.

Into this life of luxury came a visitor. When his Jewish brother Hanani came to Shushan, Nehemiah had just two questions for Hanani: "How are the Jewish people?" and "How is Jerusalem?" The questions he asked revealed a lot about his heart. Nehemiah's primary concern was not for himself or his own reputation. He didn't even express concern for his brother Hanani. Nehemiah's main concern was for the people of God and the city of God. Nehemiah understood that the reputation of God was bound up in the welfare of his people and the welfare of his city.

Nehemiah lived in the 40s and 30s, that is, the 440s and 430s B.C. He had a clear and focused understanding of the unique purpose of the Jewish people. Israelites were destined to connect the people of the world with the reality of God. Nehemiah was concerned about the welfare of the Jewish people.

Nehemiah was also concerned about Jerusalem. He loved and missed his hometown. He believed, with King David, that Jerusalem was "the joy of the whole earth . . . the city of the Great King" (Ps 48:2). He lived in Shushan, but Jerusalem was the city of his God and King. King David had united the tribes of Israel into one nation in

Jerusalem. It was the political and spiritual capital of the nation. "How are things in Jerusalem? How is my hometown? How is the city of God?"

Hanani gave a grim report. The beloved city was in ruins, its gates burned down, its walls destroyed. Without walls the city had no security, no protection from enemies. New Yorkers had the sense on September 11 that we lived in a city without walls. Where was the security? Where was our protection?

Nehemiah asked what was on his heart. "How are my people? How are the Jews?"

Hanani again had no good news to offer. "The Israelites who survived the captivity are beside themselves with anguish. They are mocked by their neighbors. There is no fear of God in the land. They have taken foreign wives and worshiped foreign gods. Both the city and the people are in ruins!"

Nehemiah cared enough to ask. He was living in the lap of luxury. He could have easily ignored the plight of the Israelites. But he cared enough to ask. How concerned are we with the plight of the people of God in our cities? How concerned are we with the condition of the city we live in? Do we care enough to ask? We cannot pray until we know how to ask. Bishop Kaufman lived in the Bronx. He asked the people of the Bronx how they were doing. He cared enough to ask, to pray and to be used by God to meet their needs.

---

2. YOU WILL NEVER LEARN TO PRAY UNTIL YOU ARE MOVED ENOUGH TO WEEP.

Nehemiah stood in shocked silence as Hanani gave the report. He was devastated. As Hanani finished speaking, Nehemiah's response was immediate, strong and compassionate. He sat down. He wept. He mourned. He fasted. He prayed.

One might understand any one of these responses. Two might even be appropriate. But Nehemiah did five things upon hearing the awful news. His strength sapped, he fell to his seat. Tears flowed unheeded down his face. He mourned over the city and the people he loved. He abstained from eating and drinking. Nehemiah, just steps from the finest kitchen in the country, with access to the king's choicest foods and wines, went without food or drink. Most important, he prayed.

The words of Hanani met Nehemiah's ears like the report of a national disaster or the sudden death of a loved one. Every American alive in the 1960s remembers where they were when they heard President John F. Kennedy had been assassinated. Everyone alive in September 2001 can recollect the horror of hearing that the World Trade Center had been attacked. I vividly remember where I was when I got the crushing news that my mother had died. Likewise, Nehemiah had received the jolt of a lifetime. He sat stunned. He was inconsolable with the unacceptable reality that God's people and God's city were in ruins.

What causes us to weep? Why do we mourn? When we look across the landscape of our cities and communities we see profound brokenness. In every major urban area of the world we are confronted with an AIDS epidemic, homelessness, youth violence, unemployment, and addiction. The AIDS epidemic in Africa is the single worst global health epidemic in 700 years, affecting more than 22 million people. When we hear of the condition of our city, do we weep?

I once asked an African American pastor how his church could sustain two semiannual sixty-hour prayer vigils—Thursday morning through Saturday night. What could there possibly be to pray about for that length of time? (I was new in the city.) The pastor explained that he had members with children in prison, people who were unemployed and could not pay their bills, and others facing serious health issues. They were in desperate situations and cried out to God for help hour after hour. Their needs were great, and their dependence on God was even greater.

Nehemiah set an example for us. He wept, prayed and fasted over the brokenness of Jerusalem. Do we weep over the spiritual and physical brokenness of our communities? Do we fast and pray to concentrate on the overwhelming needs of our world? God used Nehemiah to rebuild walls of Jerusalem. God is using present-day Nehemiahs, like Gerald Kaufman, to rebuild our cities. God can use you.

---

3. YOU WILL NEVER LEARN TO PRAY UNTIL YOU ARE HONEST ENOUGH TO CONFESS.

Forgive me, Lord. Have mercy, O God. I have sinned against you. Nehemiah confesses with a deep sense of his own sin. He confesses on behalf of the Israelites, but he also confesses his own sins. He begins by acknowledging the God to whom he is praying. "Then I said: 'O LORD, God of heaven, the great and awesome God, who keeps his covenant of love with those who love him and obey his commands . . .' " (Neh 1:5).

Nehemiah described God as Abraham did when Abraham sent his servant to find Isaac a wife. When the servant asked how he would know which young woman was the one for Isaac to marry, Abraham replied, "The God of heaven will show you who she is" (see Gen 24:7). The God of heaven is the God who is everywhere present. Abraham knew that. Nehemiah knew that.

Nehemiah's prayer was God-centered. He refers to God thirty-four times in this short prayer. Nehemiah's focus is on his Lord, and as he focuses on God, he becomes more and more aware of his own sin and his need for confession.

Before "the God of heaven" Nehemiah confesses that his people have sinned, have broken their covenant with God, are corrupt and have been unfaithful. They have broken the most important law of all, God's law. Nehemiah includes himself in the confessional. He understands that God looks at not just the individual life of the believer but also at the corporate life of the faith community.

God sent Israel into exile because it had assimilated into the surrounding culture by participating in the idolatry of the people around them. Israel was called to stand out, to be the people of God in every generation. Israel was called to be different, to uphold the laws of God. However, instead of influencing the culture around them, Israel was influenced by the surrounding culture. Instead of leading others to God, they allowed themselves to be led away from God.

Nehemiah confessed the sin of conformity. Five centuries later the apostle Paul warned the Roman church, "Do not be conformed to this world, but be transformed by the renewing of your mind, that you may prove what is that good and acceptable and perfect will of God" (Rom 12:2 NKJV).

If we are to influence our culture for Christ, we need to stand out. Too often we have blended in, integrating into the surrounding culture. We too are in need of confession. In many ways we have adopted a middle-class value system that gives priority to material possessions at the expense of sharing God's concern for broken communities and sharing God's resources with broken people. As the people of God in this generation, we are called to transform our culture by upholding the laws of God in the cities of God.

Nehemiah stakes his prayer on the promise God gave Moses in Deuteronomy 30:4. God had promised that returning to him would result in his returning his people to his city. So Nehemiah claims the promises of God. He prays in faith, envisioning a day when God's people will once again worship in his temple. His vision of a worshiping community in the city of Jerusalem fills the horizon of his praying imagination.

---

4. YOU WILL NEVER LEARN TO PRAY UNTIL YOU ARE BOLD ENOUGH TO RISK.

Nehemiah describes himself as God's servant. In fact, he uses the word *servant* eight times in the first chapter of Nehemiah. There is no question about who has authority in Nehemiah's life. Nehemiah is the servant of God. He does not refer to himself as the king's servant, although that is also true. Nehemiah's primary relationship is to "the God of heaven," and God is in charge. Nehemiah also refers to Moses as a servant and to the Israelites as servants. A servant does not question his or her master but obediently carries out the master's commands. Nehemiah exhibits a willingness to carry out the will of God, even if it means risking his own life.

Nehemiah's prayer highlights the relationship between serving God and fearing God. Nehemiah asks God to hear his prayer and the prayer of all "who desire to fear Your name" (Neh 1:11 NKJV). It is the type of fear attributed to Abraham in Genesis 22 when he took his only son, Isaac, and prepared to sacrifice him on an altar. As Abraham raised his arm, wielding a knife to kill his son, he was intercepted by an angel who spoke for God: "Now I know that you fear God, because you have not withheld from me your son, your only son" (Gen 22:12).

Fearing God contains within it a willingness to lose everything for the sake of God's reputation. Abraham was willing to slay Isaac to obey God. Moses was willing to incur the wrath of God as a substitute for Israel. Nehemiah was willing to risk his life on behalf of God's people. Christians in today's cities, both in the United States and overseas, may face serious risks not really so different from these.

Nehemiah begins his prayer with worship and adoration, moves to confession and finishes with petition. Nehemiah has three requests of God in this prayer:

He asks God to be attentive.
He asks God to remember his own promises.
He asks God to grant him success in the presence of the king.

> "It's not that we are to seek out harm. We are merely not to take ourselves so far out of harm's way in the name of security and progress that we remove God's primary strategy for reaching the city: his church."
>
> RANDY WHITE, JOURNEY TO THE CENTER OF THE CITY

If God failed to answer request number three, it could cost Nehemiah his life.

Nehemiah was the king's right-hand man. He acted as wine taster, bodyguard and advisor. He occupied an important and trustworthy position on the king's staff. Nehemiah was expected to look joyful in the king's presence at all times. He needed to "put on a happy face" even if he was crying inside. In addition, he was not to approach the king unless he was summoned. As Esther had told Mordecai, "For any man or woman who approaches the king in the inner court without being summoned the king has but one law: that he be put to death" (Esther 4:11). Appear sad before the king: risk death. Approach the king without being called: risk death.

Nehemiah approached the king only after four months of prayer and fasting (between November and March). Nehemiah's faith grew as he trusted God in prayer. He had discerned exactly what he would need to do if he was going to see the city of God rebuilt and the people of God delivered from their humiliating circumstances.

PRAYER AND STRATEGY

Nehemiah knew that he would not be successful without prayer. He also knew that he would not be successful with prayer alone. He did not pray and wait for God to act. He prayed and then acted, as he was led by God. Nehemiah employed an emotional and tactical strategy to solicit the king's support for rebuilding Jerusalem.

Emotional strategy. Although he was expected to look happy in the king's presence, he chose to look sad. He knew that his sadness would catch the king's attention. In the first two verses of Nehemiah 2, his sadness is mentioned three times. He chose not to mask his feelings, and he took a great risk. Nehemiah did not act without fear; he acted in spite of his fear. In doing so he showed immense trust in God and great courage. He allowed his sadness to show, even though he was "very much afraid" (Neh 2:2).

Nehemiah's sadness provides the opening he needs to tell the king what is on his heart. His boss, King Artaxerxes, asks him why he looks so sad when he is not ill. Nehemiah pours out his grief before the king. He appeals to the king's compassion as he tells him that the city where his fathers are buried is in ruins. King Artaxerxes had only recently issued an edict that the walls of Jerusalem should not be rebuilt (see Ezra 4:19-20). In a wisdom born in prayer, Nehemiah does not name Jerusalem but appeals to the king by referring to his ancestors' graves. Knowing that reverence for deceased relatives is strong in Middle Eastern culture, he wisely applies this knowledge to the way he words his request.

Tactical strategy. The king does not mince words. "What do you want?" he asks. What an opening! Nehemiah could not have hoped for a better response. It gave him a wide-open opportunity to lay out his plans. But before he asks the king anything, Nehemiah prays. Picture a brief *Help me, Lord!* kind of prayer. The words of the prayer are not written in the book of Nehemiah, only the fact that he "prayed to the God of heaven" (Neh 2:4). Nehemiah asks the king for permission to return to Jerusalem to rebuild the city. He is ready to give the king a specific time frame for when he will be gone and when he will return.

Nehemiah was prepared. He understood the power of advance decision making. His praying had led him to know the mind of God regarding the specific strategy of traveling to Jerusalem during a specific time. He was prepared to respond to the king's questions. The four months he spent in prayer prepared him to respond to the king.

Nehemiah had done his homework. He knew he would need political permission to travel and physical resources to rebuild the city. So he asked for it all. And God abundantly answered Nehemiah's prayer, as the king granted him everything that he requested.

At the end of chapter 2, Nehemiah returns to the three great themes from chapter one:

Who is God? He is the God of heaven.

Who are we? We are the servants of God.

What is the crisis at hand? The city gates are in ruins.

What propels the process is Nehemiah's call for united action. He did not just pray; he prayed and he acted. He did not act alone; he called on the Jews, the priests, the nobles and the officials to come alongside and assist in the rebuilding. He identified with the people when he urged them, "Come, let *us* rebuild the wall of Jerusalem, and *we* will no longer be in disgrace" (Neh 2:17, emphasis added). They responded in kind, "Let us start rebuilding" (v. 18).

By examining Nehemiah's leadership style we learn the necessary foundations for transformational change in a city. Nehemiah models great *spiritual concern* for God's people and God's city as it is expressed in prayer. Nehemiah demonstrates *servant leadership* that is willing to take life-risking steps. Nehemiah aggressively pursues the necessary *resources* needed to rebuild a city in ruins.

The motto of the Council of Leadership Foundations, active in more than fifty cities, is simply this: To get anything done, it takes leadership and it takes money. In order to do anything significant for God on a citywide scale, we must have at least three ingredients:

• the necessary *spiritual* capacity, gained through Bible study and prayer

• the necessary *leadership* capacity, gained through mentoring and experience

• the necessary *programmatic* capacity, gained through financial resources

NEHEMIAH REBUILDS JERUSALEM

Nehemiah inspires the Jewish people to work. He lists the gates of Jerusalem and the builders by name. As people get involved in the work of rebuilding, their faith is simultaneously rebuilt. Just as Nehemiah has become an answer to his own prayer, the people of Jerusalem become a solution to their own problems.

The project doesn't go smoothly. Nehemiah faces significant opposition from both within and without. He is opposed from outside by Sanballat and Tobiah. Sanballat, a Horonite, mocks and ridicules the Jews, calling them feeble. Inside the city, Nehemiah faces opposition from within his own ranks. The Jewish people complain that their fellow Jews are being enslaved and that the economy is suffering—they don't have enough food and have to mortgage their land. Nehemiah challenges the Jewish people to view their countrymen as brothers to serve, not as people to exploit.

"God's methods for the church are prayer and persuasion. But today in large segments of the church those methods are laughed at as being hopelessly inadequate, and what is offered up instead are power, politics and money."

JAMES MONTGOMERY BOICE, *TWO CITIES, TWO LOVES*

Nehemiah faces continuing opposition from Sanballat, who plans a conspiracy and tries to strike fear in Nehemiah so he will give up the work (Neh 6). Instead, Nehemiah calls on God and prays that God will strengthen his hands. Nehemiah and the workers persevere despite the tremendous discouragement and distractions.

The wall is rebuilt—miraculously, in only fifty-two days! This is an astounding achievement given the physical and spiritual condition of the city as described in chapter 1. Nehemiah was concerned enough to ask, moved enough to weep, honest enough to confess and bold enough to risk. One man's passion for God greatly affected the future of a people and a city.

What was the result of the wall being built? The surrounding nations heard about the accomplishment and discerned that God was behind it all. God was obviously concerned about Jerusalem and the Jewish people. In his sovereign wisdom he led Nehemiah to pray—and then to become an answer to his own prayer. God uses unexpected vessels to accomplish his purposes.

PRINCIPLES OF LEADERSHIP

Nehemiah's leadership can be summarized in the following ways:

- He saw God's people and God's city from God's perspective. That perspective informed the way that he prayed and acted.

• He identified with the plight of God's people through confession.

• He was more concerned about God's reputation than the comfort and longevity of his own life. He was subsequently willing to take great risks.

• Nehemiah used his unique position in the king's court to access necessary political and physical resources to serve God's people.

• Nehemiah mobilized God's people and persevered through much opposition and distraction to accomplish an enormous challenge in record time

REBUILDING HARLEM

Just as God used Nehemiah to rebuild Jerusalem, he is able to rebuild our cities when we seek him. The year was 1986. The place was Harlem. The man God used was Rev. Preston Washington. Rev. Washington was grieved by the rapidly deteriorating conditions of Harlem. More than 100,000 people had moved out of Harlem in the previous decade, leaving behind abandoned and burned-out buildings and increasingly unsafe neighborhoods. Equally disturbing was the division that had occurred among the four hundred churches in Harlem. Just like Nehemiah, Preston Washington grieved over the condition of the city and the people.

In his grief, Rev. Washington started to pray. He organized a group of pastors to meet once a month for prayer. For thirteen months pastors met monthly to repent over their disunity and take an offering for the community. Sound familiar? Begin with prayer and confession, then begin to amass resources. After thirteen prayer meetings, more than $100,000 had been collected.

With that seed money, the churches formed the Harlem Congregations for Community Improvement (HCCI) to minister to the underserved of Harlem. Over the next fifteen years, HCCI grew to include the participation of more than ninety congregations from the Harlem community. Their ministries to the real needs of the residents of Harlem include after-school programs, job training, AIDS ministries and dozens of other efforts. A primary effort of HCCI has been the provision of affordable housing for Harlem residents.

Since its inception, more than $200 million has been spent on housing renovations in the Bradhurst section of Harlem. It is estimated that within two years all of the currently abandoned housing in Harlem will be renovated. In this community of 400,000, such a program is a miracle that equals the rebuilding of the walls in Jerusalem in fifty-two days! God used Nehemiah to lead in the rebuilding of Jerusalem in the 440s B.C. God used Rev. Preston Washington to rebuild Harlem in the A.D. 1990s. God is still using those with a passion for his people and his cities to rebuild cities—for his glory.

QUESTIONS FOR REFLECTION OR DISCUSSION

1. What are the four conditions of meaningful prayer?
2. How did Nehemiah prepare for his meeting with the king?
3. What principle of leadership would you like to incorporate into your life? Ask God to work in your life in that area.

Next step: Find out about the needs in your community by attending a local community board meeting or town hall meeting. Begin to pray regularly for a specific concern in your community: high school dropouts, teenage pregnancy, unemployment or another crucial problem.

7

FOR ALL THE SAINTS
Paul and the Ephesian Christians

Just as the church in New York was praying before 9/11, the church in Ohio was praying before May 4, 1970. In case you were not alive then or do not remember its significance, May 4, 1970, is the day Kent State University grabbed the international spotlight after a tragic end to a student demonstration against the Vietnam War. But students had been praying before the tragedy struck.

In the fall of 1969, Campus Crusade for Christ, InterVarsity, Navigators and other groups met together at Grace Baptist Church to plan a campuswide student outreach. The Rev. David Bryant, who was pastor of Grace Baptist at the time, says, "Our church was a neutral meeting ground in which different streams could come together to reach the campus in a major way."[1]

In mid-April 1970—just a few weeks before the shootings—a one-week evangelistic campaign was the impetus for four hundred students receiving Christ. In early May the Christian students were preparing to follow up with the new believers when their efforts were cut short.

Shortly after noon on that Monday, thirteen seconds of rifle fire by twenty-eight Ohio National Guardsmen left four students dead, one paralyzed and eight others wounded. Some students were walking to and from class and got caught in the crossfire. Bryant explained, "The campus shut down for the remainder of the year, and we couldn't find the same students in the fall. We felt that there was a spiritual battle behind all of this."

But just as revival has been growing out of the rubble of the World Trade Center, the first fruits of revival sprang up at Kent State University after the shootings. During the next four years "our prayers were answered way beyond anything we could have imagined. We learned how to work together," said Bryant.

As these Christians sat in Grace Baptist Church, still in shock over the tragic deaths of four students, they decided to pray. Standard everyday prayers were not called for; desperate, crying-out-to-God prayers were the order of the day. David Bryant called for people to join him in prayer every week, four nights a week, two hours a night, for six weeks. This was "beyond the depth of anything I had done before," he says. A small group of eight committed intercessors commenced to pray through the book of Ephesians, reading and praying through one chapter every week for the next six weeks.

As they prayed through the book of Ephesians, the motto of the church was amended to add four words: "applying the gospel of Christ to the world of Kent *and the world beyond*." Praying through the book of Ephesians, with its emphasis on multiculturalism, opened their eyes to the world beyond that needed prayer.

Over the next several years David Bryant led prayer gatherings in 350 cities around the world (75 of those cities outside the United States), sharing his vision of encountering God through united prayer. David was instrumental in reawakening the prayer movement in the United States in the 1980s by reminding the church in America of Jonathan Edwards's vision in 1747: the church would experience revival as it came together in *visible unity* and *explicit agreement*.

In 1991 David and his family moved to the New York metro area to be closer to the emerging prayer movement in the region. He wanted to live near the prayer movement, learn from it and serve it in any way possible. He has been like a spiritual father to the prayer movement in the New York region, describing it as the most sophisticated expression of urban prayer anywhere in the world.

PAUL'S PRAYER FOR THE EPHESIANS

Toward the end of his life, the apostle Paul was sitting in a Roman prison. During this time, Paul wrote several letters, most notably Ephesians, Philippians, Colossians and Philemon. Prison is awful, but it does offer one precious commodity: time. Paul had time to reflect on his life and ministry, and the "prison epistles" are more reflective and philosophical than some of Paul's other writings. In Ephesians Paul gives an overview of the gospel, and he answers the question, What is God's purpose for this world?

The letter to the Ephesians can be divided into two parts. The first half focuses on worship and prayer, and the second half focuses on personally living for God in personal purity, marriage, parenting and evangelism. In chapter 1, Paul outlines the spiritual blessings of the believer. God the Father predestined us in eternity past; God the Son has saved us in eternity present through his blood on the cross; God the Spirit has sealed us in eternity future for our inheritance in Christ.

Paul is thankful to God for the Ephesians, for they demonstrate "love for all the saints" (Eph 1:15). Paul prays for the Ephesians, that they would know God better, that they would know their inheritance, and that they would know God's power—the same power that raised Jesus Christ from the dead. He prays for the believers in the city of Ephesus to have increased knowledge, increased hope and increased power. Paul's prayer serves as a model as we pray for our cities—as we pray for the "saints" in Chicago, or Los Angeles, or St. Louis, or Miami.

Paul concludes his prayer in chapter 1 by stating that the church is the fullness of Christ. Christ fills the church today, just as his glory filled Solomon's temple. As the church fulfills its destiny to be united before God, Christ dwells in the church—and in a city united in prayer. As the church fulfills its role, it represents Christ in the world, in our cities, in our communities.

A united New York City church met on February 5, 1988. David Bryant led a concert of prayer that included a panorama of saints from Africa, China, Korea, several parts of Latin America, Europe, India and many other nations. For many who had spent their entire lives in churches where everyone shared the same language and complexion, worshiping in unity with folks who were different was an awakening to the body of Christ in all its fullness.

As people prayed together, their eyes were opened to the reality that their new prayer partners, who looked very different from them and perhaps spoke a different language, would be their brothers and sisters for eternity. David Bryant led prayers for the adoration of God, the awakening of the church and the advancement of the gospel. Knowing the love of Christ *with all the saints* became a wonderful reality.

In chapter 2, Paul paints a vivid picture of what humanity is by nature, in contrast to what we can become by grace.[2] Paul reminds the Ephesians that they were dead, enslaved and condemned like all humans, until Christ redeemed them by his grace. Paul reminds the Ephesians, and us, that they were separated from God, "without hope and without God in the world" (Eph 2:12). And just as believers have been reconciled to God, we have also been reconciled to each other. We are now "fellow citizens" and "members of God's household" (Eph 2:19).

Jews and Gentiles who were hostile to each other are now united in Christ. Slaves and free are one in Christ. All the dividing walls have been demolished by the death of Christ on the cross. We are reconciled not just to God but to each other. Chinese and Koreans lay aside their historical dislike, and blacks and whites agree to overcome their legacy of mistrust and racism.

Most individual churches cannot experience the oneness in Christ that Paul speaks of in Ephesians, because too often our churches are monocultural, monolingual and monoracial. It is only when we meet with the broader body of Christ in our cities, when churches join together with other churches, that our oneness in Christ is truly demonstrated, to ourselves and to a watching world.

Look closely at Ephesians 2:22. Once again the Bible answers the question, What is the power of a city at prayer? The purpose of the church is to be a community in whom the Holy Spirit dwells. We are "being built together to become a dwelling in which God lives by his Spirit." Praise God. As the church unites in prayer, God dwells among us and his power is manifest. The power of a city at prayer is the power of God dwelling in a city. Yes, he *will* come and dwell with us as we call on him, united in prayer. John Stott puts it well in *God's New Society:*

> I wonder if anything is more urgent today, for the honour of Christ and for the spread of the gospel, than that the church should be, and should be seen to be, what by God's purpose and Christ's achievement it already is—a single new humanity, a model of human community, a family of reconciled brothers and sisters who love their Father and love each other, *the evident dwelling place of God by his Spirit.* Only then will the world believe in Christ as Peacemaker. Only then will God receive the glory due to His name.[3]

There is urgency, then, in uniting the body of Christ in our cities.

Only as we unite will God's purpose for the church be fulfilled, that the world will know that Christ is indeed Lord.

One of the beautiful things about this unity is that it doesn't change the individual. As we unite, we don't relinquish our distinctiveness; we don't abandon our differences; we don't attempt to assimilate. As we unite, we bring all of our own unique traits to contribute to the larger church. Some bring a commitment to early morning prayer; others bring a desire to pray in tongues; others bring a longing for quiet, contemplative prayer. Uniting in prayer doesn't obliterate the differences in the body of Christ. Unity helps us appreciate the differences even more.

At the beginning of a concert of prayer we often recite a statement of unity. Reading in unison, we agree to appreciate each other and each unique expression of love for God; we covenant to not be offended by how another person worships or prays; and we submit to each other in sensitivity. On many occasions when David Bryant leads large prayer gatherings he asks people to call out their denominational affiliation. You might hear, "Lutheran . . . Baptist . . . charismatic . . . A.M.E. . . . Mennonite . . . Pentecostal . . . Presbyterian." For an evening, what has divided us for centuries is surrendered to the greater cause of unity in Christ.

In the third chapter of Ephesians Paul makes his strongest statement about the church's relationship to Christ and to the world. The major lesson taught by Paul in Ephesians 3 is the biblical centrality of the church.[4] The church is central in human history; it is central to the gospel; and the church is central in Christian living.[5] The church is the mystery of God in the world. The greatest mystery of all is that the physical body of Christ had to be broken so that the worldwide body of Christ could become one.

In Paul's second prayer he pours out his spirit before God. The desire of Paul's heart is that the Ephesian church would be strengthened with might and that Christ would dwell in their hearts. Paul grasped perhaps the greatest paradox of the universe: the God of creation takes up residence in the human heart. Our hearts are Christ's home.

Paul continues to pray that the Ephesians would be "rooted and grounded in love." They should be like a well-planted tree, with love as the fruit. They should be like a well-built house, with love as the foundation.

The next part of Paul's prayer is crucial to understanding the importance of a united, praying church. He prays that the church would know the love of Christ, but he states that they will only know the love of Christ in all its dimensions as they know it *"with all the saints."* We can't do it alone. We can't fully experience the love of God in isolation. If there is no other reason to unite with others in prayer, this is the reason. If you want to experience the love of Christ in all its fullness, you must be united with other believers. It is not optional—it is imperative. Paul's prayer about grasping the love of Christ (Eph 3:17-19) is based on our making every effort—not *some* effort, but *every* effort.

As we evaluate our own use of time, how much time do we spend in the actual promotion of unity, bringing diverse people together? At the root of this command is the understanding that Christianity is not a program but an environment, an environment of relationship. When the environment is right, individuals and churches will be reproducing themselves.

We cannot possibly comprehend the love of Christ with our limited human understanding, but we will approach a fuller understanding of Christ's love as we join together with all the saints. Christ's love reaches out in every direction, to every person. His love is broad enough to reach all humanity; his love is long enough to last for eternity; his love is high enough to take us to heaven; his love is deep enough to forgive the unforgivable.

We understand Christ's love as we unite with all the saints. We need each other. The white church is incomplete without the black church. The Japanese church is incomplete without the Korean church. The Latino church is incomplete without the Chinese church. We are incomplete without one another.

One of the most powerful emotional experiences this side of heaven is to be loved by someone who is completely different from us. At each of our Pastors' Prayer Summits we intentionally share Communion with someone who is different from us. This simple expression of unity illustrates the love of God in Christ, who reached down to us who are so much lower than he. John Stott describes the church as "God's new society":

> The church as a multi-racial, multi-cultural community is like a beautiful tapestry. Its members come from a wide range of colourful backgrounds. No other human community resembles it. Its diversity and harmony are unique. It is God's new society. And the many-coloured fellowship of the church is a reflection of the many-coloured wisdom of God.[6]

Paul concludes his prayer with the affirmation that God can do immeasurably more than we could ever ask or imagine, "according to his power that is at work within us" (Eph 3:20). The power that is at work within us refers to both individuals and the broader body of Christ. Individually, God dwells in our hearts by faith; corporately, God dwells among his people. Once again we are reminded that the power of a city at prayer is God dwelling in the city because his people are united in prayer!

David Bryant did not know that his earth-shattering experience in Kent, Ohio, would lead him into a global prayer ministry. He did not know that a missions trip to India would result in the adoption of three precious Indian children. He never imagined that a prayer of consecration would produce an invitation to speak to a million men on the mall in Washington, D.C. God has done more than David Bryant asked or imagined when he prayed through the book of Ephesians. And as we gather in prayer in our cities, he will do more in them than we can ever ask or imagine—for his glory.

PRINCIPLES FOR LIVING

Paul lays out God's eternal purposes in the first three chapters, and then he proceeds to exhort the church by laying down principles for living. Foundational to living for Christ is living in unity. It is not negotiable; it is not optional; it is not voluntary. We must "make every effort to keep the unity of the Spirit through the bond of peace" (Eph 4:3). Paul expands on the theme of Jesus' prayer in John 17 that the church would be one so that the world might believe.

Unity is central to the gospel. Unity breeds belief, and disunity breeds atheism. Unity can only happen when we are reconciled to God and reconciled to each other. Disunity proclaims that God is not big enough or powerful enough or real enough to cause people to truly love one another. Either unity is our top priority or it is not even on our list. Unity takes effort, and it requires perseverance. Unity is not easy, and it is often not pretty. Unity can be uncomfortable, and it involves taking risks. But the benefits far outweigh the trials.

Paul lays out prerequisites for Christian unity: we must be humble, gentle, forbearing and patient. Paul tells the church that believers can be united, because God is a triunity. He urges the Ephesians to grow up into unity. Over the past fifteen years of the prayer movement in Greater New York, pastors and churches have learned to love one another. They didn't start out united; it has been a learning and growing experience.

> *"Prayer is political action. Prayer is social energy. Prayer is public good. Far more of our nation's life is shaped by prayer than is formed by legislation."*
>
> EUGENE PETERSON, *EARTH AND ALTAR*

Korean-speaking pastors have stepped out of their comfort zones in the Korean church and joined with English-speaking pastors in prayer. Black Pentecostal pastors have offered to refrain from speaking in tongues, so as not to offend or confuse others. Conservative Chinese pastors have been stretched as they worship alongside charismatic brothers and sisters.

As we come out of our churches, leave our comfortable places and experience unity with all the saints, we are getting a taste of heaven. We are approximating that final prayer meeting, in the city of God, when we join with all the saints: with that "great multitude that no one could count, from every nation, tribe, people and language, standing before the throne and in front of the Lamb" (Rev 7:9).

THE ARMOR OF GOD

In chapters 4-6 Paul teaches the Ephesians new principles for living, and he teaches husbands, wives, parents and children how to relate to one another and live in harmony. He concludes the book of Ephesians with that great passage on the armor of God. Conscious of the challenges facing the early church, Paul gives the Ephesian Christians a mental picture of resisting the evil one. He knew that whereas Caesar wanted to silence his witness, Satan wanted to destroy his soul.

Paul's exhortation is to put on the whole armor of God while resisting the evil one. Stand firm. He repeats this admonition several times: "take your stand"; "stand your ground"; "stand"; "stand firm then." Paul urges them to pray with alertness, to pray on the offensive and to pray for all the saints.

While leading prayer gatherings in different parts of the world, David Bryant sometimes has the participants imagine putting on the whole armor of God. He asks people to pray "the way most of the Christians pray in most parts of the world—simultaneously out loud." David exhorts them to reach up and touch the part of their body that the armor is going on.

Stop for just a moment now, and imagine with me. Reach up and touch your head as you put on the helmet of salvation; hold out your shield of faith; wield your sword of the Spirit, which is the word of God; slip your feet into the shoes of the gospel of peace; put on the belt of truth; get into the breastplate of righteousness. Do you have all the armor on? Are you ready for battle? Stay in position. Hold steady. Now pray. Pray. Pray.

Like the Christians in Ephesus of old, we too need the armor of God as we stand for him in the cities where he has placed us. Then, as we engage in united prayer, God will give victory.

QUESTIONS FOR REFLECTION OR DISCUSSION

1. How did David Bryant's small group pray through the book of Ephesians?
2. Why is unity in the body of Christ so important?
3. What prerequisites for Christian unity does Paul teach?

Next step: Find a Christian brother or sister of a different cultural background to pray with on a regular basis.

Being a Servant Leader
Barnabas

As the movie *Rain Man* opens, Charlie Babbit, played by Tom Cruise, is a selfish, self-centered, impatient young man. Although estranged from his wealthy father, when he finds out his father has died Charlie hopes to inherit millions of dollars. As the will is read, the estate, worth three million dollars, is bequeathed to an unnamed beneficiary. Charlie is furious. He receives only his dad's prized rose garden and 1949 Buick. Charlie got what his father prized the most—but not what he wanted. He felt cheated out of his birthright.

CALLED TO BE A LEVITE

In the Old Testament book of Joshua there is a reading of a will—of sorts. When Joshua was advanced in age, the Lord instructed him to divide the land and allocate to each of the twelve tribes a portion for their inheritance. Well, actually, to *eleven* of the twelve tribes. The twelfth tribe, the tribe of Levi, received no land. Joshua told them the Lord was their inheritance. Not land—the Lord. I wonder how they felt when they received the news. Were they surprised? Were they bitter? Like Charlie Babbit, they received what the Father prized most. They were called to relationship—with God and his people.

The Levites had a special calling and a special privilege. They were to serve as God's representatives before the people, and they were to represent the people before God. Theirs was a priestly calling. Moses was a Levite. He pleaded for the mercy of God after the Israelites rebelled and worshiped a golden calf. The Levites were called to be people of prayer. They were to be people who manifested a life of sacrifice. The Levites were mobilizers, networkers, encouragers—calling people around a vision for God and his purposes.

One of the most influential Levites in the early church was Barnabas. Barnabas lived up to his name—he was truly a "son of encouragement." Originally his name was Joses; the apostles added the name Barnabas to reflect his character and gift as an encourager. He encouraged the newly forming church not only by his words but by his sacrificial actions. Examining the life of Barnabas will reveal some timeless truths about the importance of ministry behind the scenes—and the priority of relationship. The twenty-first-century church still needs people like Barnabas.

A MODERN-DAY BARNABAS

Jeremy Del Rio is a modern-day Barnabas. He is an emerging leader, and although still young, he has already been a great encouragement to the body of Christ in New York City. I first met Jeremy when he was president of the InterVarsity Christian Fellowship chapter at New York University. Jeremy galvanized the nine Christian clubs on campus around a common goal: outreach. The 50,000 students at NYU needed to hear the gospel, and Jeremy knew the InterVarsity chapter could not reach the campus alone.

Under Jeremy's leadership, the nine campus fellowship groups formed the Christian Inter-Fellowship Council, which went on to produce a campus outreach event that was named the "Event of the Year" by New York University. Bruce Kuhn, a gifted Christian actor, acted out the Gospel of Luke before packed crowds of students. Jeremy noted that the "genesis for the uniting of the clubs on campus came from frustration that all the Christian clubs were small and struggling. . . . I saw a glaring need that in order to have relevance we had to work collaboratively."[1]

When he was nine years old, Jeremy heard a sermon his father preached. The message was "Alone we cannot do it—but together we can take the city for Jesus." Rev. Richard Del Rio planted seeds of cooperation and collaboration in his nine-year-old son's life. Those seeds found good ground and have produced the fruit of encouragement and relationship building.

BARNABAS: TENTMAKER

When Barnabas is first mentioned in the New Testament in Acts 4, he is shown selling his land and giving the proceeds to the apostles.[2] He did not just give lip service to the church. Barnabas demonstrated his love for the church by giving generously. And Barnabas was a tentmaker. When called into leadership, he did not want to burden the new church, so he continued supporting himself. In 1 Corinthians 9:6, Paul mentions Barnabas as setting an example by working for a living.

After graduating from NYU, Jeremy Del Rio took a year off, intending to go to Guatemala on a short-term mission. He was serving as the youth minister at his father's church. His father discouraged him from traveling, telling Jeremy he was needed at the church.[3] A brother from Texas gave Jeremy a word from the Lord: God was calling Jeremy to "be an Aaron" and hold up his father's arms in ministry.

Jeremy heeded the advice of his father and his brother in the Lord: he stayed in New York City. Working in youth ministry at the church for a year, he received no salary. Like Barnabas, he gave sacrificially.

During that year Jeremy was instrumental in forming Generation X-Cel, a youth center in housing projects on the Lower East Side of Manhattan.[4] Generation X-Cel proves that the Generation X crowd can make positive contributions to society. Youth are offered godly alternatives to street life such as after-school programs, summer day camps, computer training and community outreach. Ayana, a high school junior, puts it this way:

> One of the greatest experiences in my life was being involved in a program that empowered young children to look beyond their circumstances of living in neighborhoods full of drugs, crime and violence and encourage them to reach for their dreams. Working at Generation X-Cel this past summer was an experience I'll never forget. I was helping to keep kids off the street and engaged in activities that would benefit their future.

After launching Generation X-Cel, Jeremy attended New York University Law School for three years on a full scholarship. During law school he continued to work with youth and guide Generation X-Cel. Upon graduation, Jeremy was offered a full-time job at one of the most prestigious law firms in New York City, Dewey Ballantine, L.L.P. Although the firm wanted Jeremy to work full-time, he managed to finagle a part-time job offer so he could continue his work with youth. A twentieth-century tentmaker, not unlike the first-century Barnabas, Jeremy worked to finance his ministry. This was an unprecedented arrangement with this New York City law firm.

On September 11, Jeremy called his dad after the first plane hit the World Trade Center. He quickly realized that there were plenty of workers at Ground Zero, and his "contribution would be best behind the scenes."

By September 13, Jeremy decided to leave his secure job at Dewey Ballantine and devote himself to full-time ministry. With a wife and infant son at home to support, the decision was not made lightly, but he says, "I knew God would open up the right door." Jeremy exchanged the material security of a high-paying job for the spiritual security of serving God. Sure enough, within a week Jeremy sent off his résumé to World Vision, and soon he was hired as the community relations director.

SAUL IN THE CITY

Let's set the scene for Barnabas's unique ministry. Saul of Tarsus, a Pharisee, is traveling to Damascus to wreak havoc among believers. His goal is to find followers of "the Way," to arrest and imprison them. On the road to Damascus he is stopped in his tracks by none other than the Lord Jesus himself. It is a dramatic and history-altering conversion story. Blinded and limping, he walks into town.

As Saul waits in a house on Straight Street, the Lord sends the terrified Ananias to him to restore his sight. Picture a rabbi sent to visit Hitler. That's about how Ananias might have felt. He was going to see the man who was responsible for the persecution and arrest of Christians.

But Ananias is obedient. When he finds Saul, he puts his hand on Saul's shoulder and says two of the most tender words recorded in the New Testament: "Brother Saul." This man who had been public enemy number one was now a brother in Christ.

After Saul begins preaching and telling the Jews that Jesus is the Son of God, the Jews conspire to kill him. Fearing for his life, Saul flees to Jerusalem and attempts to join the disciples. He is not received warmly by the disciples because they are all afraid of him. The grounds for suspicion are well founded. Who would believe a man who has been responsible for the imprisonment, torture and possible death of friends and family members? Barnabas does.

BARNABAS: FRIEND OF NEWCOMERS

Barnabas comes to the rescue. He advocates for Saul, telling the disciples how fearlessly Saul has preached in Damascus. Barnabas encourages the disciples to accept Saul, and he encourages Saul to become a part of the new church in Jerusalem. If it were not for Barnabas's acceptance of Saul and his encouraging the disciples to accept Saul as well, all the missionary travels of the apostle Paul and the subsequent spread of the gospel might never have happened. Barnabas's diligent and quiet work of encouragement behind the scenes changed the whole course of church history. John Stott believes that "there is an urgent need for modern . . . Barnabases who . . . take the initiative to befriend newcomers."[5]

Another modern-day Barnabas might not have stayed in New York City if he had not received encouragement from an established pastor in the city. Glen Kleinknecht arrived in New York City in 1976. He came with Campus Crusade for Christ to help lead an evangelistic program—the I Found It campaign. This young man from Indiana did not know much about New York City, but he knew he wanted to serve God and spread the gospel.

Glen described his most humbling moment, which came shortly after he arrived in New York. At an informational meeting for pastors to describe the I Found It campaign, a pastor stood up and asked Glen, "Where are you from?"

"Indiana, by way of North Carolina," Glen replied.

The pastor then asked, "How long have you been in the city?"

The answer, "Eight days."

The message was clear: you are an outsider and you are not really welcome here.

But Glen didn't cower. Through the campaign, it became obvious to Glen that New York City was a very strategic place to do world evangelism. Glen prayed, *I'm available, Lord.* Glen looked around New York and saw practically the whole world represented there. If they were reached with the gospel, he thought, they would be key disciples going throughout the world. What a strategic and pragmatic approach to fulfilling the Great Commission!

Glen could easily have left New York after the campaign was over. But pastors like Rev. Robert Johansson of Evangel Church encouraged Glen, mentored him and advocated for him with other city leaders—much as Barnabas did for Paul. Twenty-five years later, Glen is still living and ministering in New York City.

> *"Prayer is the action that gets us in touch with and develops the most comprehensive relationship—self, God, community, creation, government, culture."*
>
> EUGENE PETERSON,
> *EARTH AND ALTAR*

BARNABAS: BENEVOLENT SERVANT

The disciples sent Barnabas to Antioch to nurture the new believers. As Barnabas witnessed the faith of the new converts and saw the grace of God evident in their lives, he was joyful and "encouraged them all to remain true to the Lord with all their hearts" (Acts 11:23). Instead of making a name for himself and building up a church that would honor him, Barnabas sought out Saul to come to Antioch and assist him in the ministry. Barnabas exemplified humility and servanthood in ministry. He knew the importance and priority of relationships.

Barnabas and Saul ministered for a year in Antioch. According to

John Stott, "They must have taught about Christ, making sure that the converts knew both the facts and the significance of his life, death, resurrection, exaltation, Spirit-gift, present reign and future coming."[6] Antioch was a walled city, and the population was divided into African, Asian, Jewish and European quarters. When people from all these communities began to follow Jesus, the citizens of Antioch didn't know what to call this diverse group of people. So they named the believers "Christ-ians," or "little Christs."

During this time a famine hit parts of the region, and the church at Antioch quickly raised up a famine relief fund to assist the church in Jerusalem. Barnabas and Saul carried the money to the Jerusalem church. Paul himself refers to this visit in his letter to the Galatians. Paul writes that the apostles urged him to "continue to remember the poor, the very thing I was eager to do" (Gal 2:10). Barnabas both encouraged the church spiritually and helped provide for the physical needs of the church. He showed a special concern and commitment to the poor and needy.

Glen Kleinknecht has played a Barnabas role during his twenty-five years of ministry in New York. He and the staff of Here's Life Inner City minister in New York by coming alongside churches and assisting pastors in their ministry. One example of their ministry is the Boxes of Love campaign. Each year at Thanksgiving hundreds of volunteers pack boxes with a complete Thanksgiving dinner to be distributed to the poor in communities across the city. In 1996 a warehouse was purchased in Queens to serve as a launching pad for receiving donations and distributing food products to churches to enable them to serve the poor.

As Glen has ministered among the poor for more than two decades, the truth of James 2:5 has come to life: "Has not God chosen those who are poor in the eyes of the world to be rich in faith and to inherit the kingdom he promised those who love him?" Glen says that by hanging out with the poor, he has learned more about faith in God. He believes that the ingredient that causes their faith to be strong and dynamic is the very thing that repels most of us: their desperation. Poor folks are desperate, and their desperation leads them to a greater need: a yearning, a longing for God to show up in their lives.

World Vision is a Barnabas-type organization. The organization exists to serve the poor and youth in communities around the world. On September 13, 2001, I was approached by World Vision to help create a relief fund to assist victims of the World Trade Center disaster. Just as Barnabas and Saul went to Jerusalem to assist the struggling church there, World Vision wanted to come to New York and assist the devastated church here. The American Families Assistance Fund (AFAF) was created, and six million dollars was raised from concerned Christians desiring to bless New Yorkers.

The AFAF helped provide trauma counseling training for thousands of pastors and lay ministers; it provided food resources for street ministry and prayer booths for prayer ministry. Thousands of people who lost their jobs or their spouses when the towers came crashing down have received financial assistance. The victims receive their checks in neighborhood churches; a World Vision staff member and the pastor present the check and offer to pray for the victim. In some ways, it would be much easier to send checks through the mail. But this would bypass the relational touch, the human-to-human contact that promotes healing. Through the warm personal connection of picking up their checks in local churches, some people have received Christ, and others have renewed their commitment to Christ and the church.

BARNABAS: SENT BY THE HOLY SPIRIT

Barnabas and Saul returned to Antioch after they distributed the famine relief funds to the church in Jerusalem. The scene in Acts 13 depicts the leaders of the early church at Antioch, described as prophets and teachers, worshiping the Lord and fasting. This was an eclectic group of ministers. Simeon, called Niger, was a black African; Lucius of Cyrene was North African; Manaen was a member of Herod's court; Barnabas was a Levite from Cyprus; Saul was a Jew from Tarsus. These five men embodied the ethnic and cultural diversity of Antioch, and they serve as an example of leadership in an ethnically diverse setting.

A message came from the Holy Spirit: "Set apart for me Barnabas and Saul for the work to which I have called them" (Acts 13:2). It is interesting to note that Barnabas is mentioned first, which is very likely a sign of his importance. Barnabas was a very important figure in the early church, although none of his sermons are recorded and he did not write any epistles. Barnabas worked tirelessly behind the scenes, encouraging new believers, preaching to the unbelievers and bringing the church together.

Just as the church itself was birthed in a prayer meeting (Acts 1—2), the international mission of the church was also birthed in a prayer meeting. The Bible passage does not describe how the message of the Holy Spirit was delivered, only that it was the Holy Spirit directing them. The call itself was also vague. God did not tell them to go to a specific area—he did not say "go to Cyprus" or "go to Rome." First they fasted and prayed. Then Barnabas and Saul stepped out in faith, and thus began the first missionary journey of the Christian church.

When God calls us to follow him, he doesn't always make it immediately clear *where* we are to go. Seeking his will through prayer, reading the Scriptures, asking the advice of godly friends and discerning the importance of circumstances can all lead us to a clearer picture of God's will for our lives. Jeremy Del Rio felt that God was calling him to serve in Guatemala for the summer. But a combination of circumstances and the counsel of a brother in the Lord caused him to stay in New York. Countless young people have been ministered to through Generation X-Cel, which would not have been started if Jeremy had gone to Guatemala.

Glen Kleinknecht was on his way to North Africa. He too felt the call of God on his life, and he felt compelled to share Christ with Muslims in North Africa. New York City was just a stopover. He came to help out with a campaign, but his final destination was North Africa. God has a unique way of steering our lives in our service to him. Again, because of a combination of the advice of godly colleagues and the sense that God was at work in New York, Glen put down roots in New York City, raised his family here and has been instrumental in leading many to Christ over the past twenty-five years.

BARNABAS: COMPANION

The relationship between Barnabas and Saul up to this point was that of Barnabas the mentor and Saul the disciple. During the first missionary journey the relationship changed. Saul, soon to be called Paul, began to take center stage as he became a missionary leader, and Barnabas, his mentor and companion, took a back seat. Later on in the book of Acts, the prominence changed further. From this point on, when the two men are mentioned together Paul is usually named first—Barnabas and Saul becomes Paul and Barnabas. There is no indication that Barnabas's ministry became any less effective when Paul became the public speaker and apologist. The faithful support role Barnabas played, and his continuing prayers, were absolutely crucial in Saul's going on to become the great apostle Paul.

Barnabas was adaptable, and he was flexible—two qualities that are necessary in the life of someone with a ministry of encouragement. Jeremy Del Rio is comfortable speaking in Spanish on the streets of the Lower East Side in Manhattan or conversing in English with government officials at City Hall. Glen Kleinknecht is at ease hanging out with homeless men at the Bowery Mission or leading a group of businessmen on a Vision Tour of the various ministries in New York City. To be effective as a mentor, networker and encourager, one must demonstrate the ability to go with the flow—to be flexible and adaptable.

THE IMPORTANCE OF FORGIVENESS

The last glimpse of Barnabas can be seen in Acts 15. Paul wanted to go and revisit all the cities they had previously visited. He wanted to encourage the new churches and make sure their faith was strong and grounded on truth. Barnabas wanted to take along a fellow minister in the faith, John Mark. Paul was still upset with John Mark, as he had deserted Paul and Barnabas in Pamphylia. But Barnabas was adamant in his defense of John Mark, wanting to give him a second chance. They split up, Barnabas traveling with John Mark and Paul leaving with Silas. This is the last mention of Barnabas in the books of Acts. He continued his ministry of encouragement to the end.

John Mark made some mistakes, and Paul was reluctant to work with him again. But Barnabas found it in his heart to forgive John Mark and bring him alongside in the ministry. Chuck Colson is a modern-day John Mark. He was once one of the most powerful men in America, special counsel to President Richard Nixon. After the Watergate fiasco and subsequent trial, Chuck Colson was sentenced to prison. But before his one- to three-year sentence was imposed, Chuck Colson accepted Jesus Christ as his Lord and Savior.

One of the first men to disciple Chuck Colson, Doug Coe, told Chuck that because of his new relationship with Jesus Christ former enemies would now be friends.

> Wait and see, Chuck. Wait and see. You will have brothers all over this city, hundreds of them, men and women you don't even know who will want nothing more than to help you. Some of them know we are meeting and are praying for you right now.[7]

What a beautiful picture of scores of Barnabases engaged in a ministry of encouragement—waiting to welcome a new believer, scars and all, into fellowship. Some who had worked against Chuck Colson and the Nixon administration took some persuading before welcoming Colson with open arms. Iowa Senator Harold Hughes had opposed the Nixon administration at every turn. Senator Hughes admitted, "There isn't anyone I dislike more than Chuck Colson."[8] After a planned get-together between Colson and Senator Hughes at which Colson gave his testimony, Senator Hughes embraced Colson and told him, "You have accepted Jesus and he has forgiven you. I do the same. I love you now as my brother in Christ."[9]

Thank God for all the Christians who advocated for Chuck Colson and welcomed him when he came out of prison. Chuck went on to start Prison Fellowship, a Barnabas-type ministry that reaches out with the gospel to inmates, ex-offenders, prisoners' families and victims of crime. Thousands and thousands of men and women have heard the gospel and been discipled by the staff and volunteers of Prison Fellowship. But the ministry of Prison Fellowship would never have come to fruition without the ministers of encouragement behind the scenes, the unnamed and unknown Barnabases.

LEARNING TO LOVE

Paul is perhaps the most well-known character in the New Testament, other than Jesus. Barnabas, though fairly prominent in the book of Acts, is far overshadowed by Paul. But Barnabas played a very important role behind the scenes, and his ministry was vital to the growth of the early church. He valued relationships—with God, with Paul, with John Mark.

Jeremy and Glen are not the most well-known Christians in New York City. Their work is often behind the scenes, a ministry of encouragement, networking, building relationships and prayer. However, like Barnabas, people like Jeremy and Glen—and ministries such as World Vision and Prison Fellowship—are essential to the growth of the church.

Most of the people whose prayers are the lifeline of a city (bringing about better circumstances, new conversions, racial reconciliation and stronger churches) will never be famous like Paul. Many "sons of encouragement" are needed to back up the work of every leader. If God is calling you to be "supporting cast," remember Barnabas, and do so joyfully.

In the film *Rain Man,* after the will is read, Charlie Babbit learns he has an autistic savant older brother, Raymond, played brilliantly by Dustin Hoffman. Charlie begins the relationship by kidnapping Raymond, hoping to extort $1.5 million from their father's estate. By the end of the movie, Charlie has learned to care deeply for his brother, and he turns down an offer of $250,000 to give up his claims of guardianship. He undergoes a transformation—from a mean-spirited, angry man into a caring brother. During his cross-country trip with Raymond he learns to encourage him rather than curse at him. He grows to love his brother. Charlie becomes a bit more like Barnabas as he learns to value what is important in life: relationships.

QUESTIONS FOR REFLECTION OR DISCUSSION

1. What was the inheritance of the Levites?
2. What two qualities are necessary in the life of someone with a ministry of encouragement?
3. Name four characteristics in Barnabas's life that led him to exemplify his name, "son of encouragement."

Next step: Identify someone in your church who has leadership potential. Begin to pray for and encourage them to follow God's call on their life.

PART THREE

LEADING PRAYER
for the
CITY

9

SOME WAYS TO PRAY

Now what? Now that you're motivated, you want to start praying with others, you're ready to go . . . now what? There are many ways to gather communities and cities in prayer. In the Metro New York region several different types of communitywide prayer have been attempted, some successfully, some not so successfully. This chapter will highlight some ways to pray as a community or city. Some initiatives will work better in smaller communities; others will work better in larger cities. But all of the prayer ideas will bring your city or town together in prayer—united prayer. And that is the goal.

Concerts of Prayer Greater New York was formed in 1997. Prior to that, I was the director of the Urban Strategy Division of Concerts of Prayer International. Having an organizational base to work out of is helpful, even necessary, for some kinds of prayer initiatives. Projects and events that require an initial outlay of money will need the backing of a church, church organization, denomination or parachurch ministry.

For instance, to plan a prayer summit for pastors will require some organizational support. A deposit will need to be made to the retreat center; brochures need to be produced and mailed; an account will have to be set up to receive the registration money. Planning a prayer walk simply requires volunteers willing to make calls and lead the walk. For each of the suggested citywide prayer initiatives listed in this chapter, starting with a small group of Christians committed to unity and procuring the support of a pastors' group or large church will make the effort succeed. The most important ingredient to success in all citywide efforts is prayer. Bathe the plans in prayer, saturate the leaders in prayer, and let the Holy Spirit guide you in prayer.

PRAYER ON HIGH

On November 18, 2000, over 100 people joined hands in prayer at the Top of the World—the 107th floor of the World Trade Center. The World Trade Center observatory was the highest outdoor viewing platform in the world until September 11, 2001. These prayer warriors were part of a Christian Community Development Association (CCDA) conference. Saturday, November 18, was designated a day of prayer for the conference, and folks from all over the country who had traveled to New York to attend the CCDA conference came to pray on top of the World Trade Center.

New York offers unique opportunities to pray atop skyscrapers that many other cities do not afford. Tragically, we can no longer pray from the Top of the World. However, we still take groups up to the top of the Empire State Building, once again the tallest building in New York City. Back in March 1997, as part of a Lord's Watch Conference, a hundred intercessors gathered at the top of the Empire State Building to pray. They used the following prayer guide as they walked around the observatory praying over the region. In each direction they prayed for the four R's of the Lord's Watch, which will be further described later in this chapter: revival, reconciliation, reformation and reaching the lost (see figure 3).

Find the highest place in your city or town you can gather at! It may be a skyscraper, a mountain or just a small hill. A prayer event in a high place can be planned as part of a larger prayer gathering, which is how it has been done in New York, or it can be an event in itself. A small committee of dedicated individuals can plan such an event by

TO THE NORTH:

Revival: for the upstate pastors' meeting on April 15.
Reconciliation: for the ethnically diverse churches of Manhattan to unite.
Reformation: for the community development work at Latino Pastoral Action Center in the South Bronx.
Reaching the Lost: for the impact of the gospel on the business community.

TO THE WEST:

Revival: for the Friday night meeting at Bethany Assembly of God.
Reconciliation: for the Sister Church movement to grow.
Reformation: for New York City Relief.
Reaching the Lost: for international students at New Jersey colleges.

TO THE EAST:

Revival: for the pastors of Queens, Long Island and Brooklyn to be revived.
Reconciliation: for the March for Jesus in Brooklyn to attract scores of churches.
Reformation: for the community development work of Greater Allen A.M.E. Cathedral of New York in Jamaica, Queens.
Reaching the Lost: for Muslims, Jews and Hindus in Queens and Brooklyn.

TO THE SOUTH:

Revival: for the Promise Keepers office here in the Empire State Building.
Reconciliation: for Chinatown churches to be united.
Reformation: for the work of the McCauley Street Mission to the homeless.
Reaching the Lost: for Wall Street leaders to be reached by Christian businessmen.

Figure 3. Praying in Four Directions

first obtaining the support of some leading pastors. Once you have a core group of committed people and the support of some of the local pastors, get the word out by all means possible:

- mailings to local churches
- advertisements in Christian newspapers and on Christian radio
- flyers in the community
- bulletin inserts given to churches
- announcements at pastors' prayer groups or denominational meetings

Ideally, one or two local churches will see the benefit of a citywide prayer effort and agree to support the initiative not only with prayer but also with finances to cover printing costs and so on.

Be creative. Don't just advertise to the Christian community. Surprisingly enough, many times unbelievers will be attracted to a prayer event, and it may even be a way to introduce them to Jesus Christ.

It is an exhilarating experience to pray from the highest place in a city, looking out over all the people God has drawn to the city, praying for the myriad ministries in the city. In some ways, it is the closest we will ever get to seeing things from God's perspective. We tend to pray only for what we can see, for the people we interact with and ministries we are involved in. Looking out over a city helps us get a bigger picture of how God is working and wants to work in our city.

PRAYER ON THE STREETS

Prayer-walking may seem like a relatively new phenomenon, but it has roots over three thousand years old. Remember Joshua leading the Israelites in a march around the city of Jericho for seven days? Although the Bible text does not specifically mention prayer, I think that during those seven days the Israelites were praying as they marched.

Steve Hawthorne has described prayer-walking as "praying on site with insight."[1] Prayer-walking is often preparatory—done before an event, in advance of an important legislative vote or prior to a major outreach effort. Prayer-walking is a way to prepare the ground for God to work, to "take back" physical places and saturate them with the presence of God, to pave the way for the Holy Spirit to work.

Before the CCDA conference, a small group of committed intercessors prayed over all five hotels that would be used during the conference and over all twenty-three ministry sites that would be visited during the conference. They prayer-walked at the church where the conference was to be held and around the top of the World Trade Center. They were preparing the ground, asking God to bless the very ground they stood on, praying for those who would soon arrive for the conference. Led by staff member Pauline Nishida, this small band of committed intercessors branched out over all the five boroughs and New Jersey, praying over every location that would be visited by the conference participants over the course of the five-day conference.

Churches can undertake prayer walks in the neighborhood around the church. It's a way to make themselves known, getting outside the four walls of the church, as well as to pray for their community and for the presence of God to be revealed. Families can prayer-walk around their houses, their apartment buildings or their neighborhood, asking God to use them as his vessels of love and grace in the community. High school students can prayer-walk around their high schools, asking God to use them and praying for boldness as they share their faith with fellow students. Business men and women can prayer-walk around their workplace and surrounding neighborhood, praying that God will help them to maintain integrity and live out their faith in the marketplace. Christian corrections officers and inmates (if allowed) can prayer-walk around the prison, pleading for the presence of God and the salvation of more officers and inmates. I think you get the idea. Prayer-walking can take place anytime, anywhere.

You can pray out loud while walking, or pray silently in your spirit. You can prayer-walk alone or with a large group of people. You can sing as you walk, pray out loud, hum or pray silently. The point is to take prayer out to the streets. Pray as you walk, and walk as you pray.

ON-SITE BEHIND-THE-SCENES PRAYER

Many churches are now seeking people to pray *for* the worship service *during* the worship service. I recently heard about a church in New Jersey where forty people are praying during the Sunday morning service every week—for the pastor, for the message, for salvation, for unity, for reconciliation. It is a powerful behind-the-scenes ministry, and those who are up front greatly appreciate knowing they are being prayed for as they minister.

The CCDA conference in November 2000 was held at New York Presbyterian Church, a large Korean church in Queens. Adjacent to the fellowship hall at New York Presbyterian is a small prayer room. After taking your shoes off, you enter the prayer room quietly and assume an attitude of prayer. During the entire CCDA conference, the room was always occupied with one to ten people praying over every aspect of the conference. As you plan citywide prayer initiatives, don't forget to have people praying for the event *during* the event. This is an often overlooked avenue of prayer.

UNITY DINNERS

One way to foster unity in a community or city is to hold a citywide or communitywide unity dinner. To eliminate costs and allow for delectable culinary diversity, ask each person to bring a dish from their home country. The result will be both delicious and unifying! Encourage people to sit at the table with folks from other churches, not just with the church members they came with. A unity dinner might have a short program after the meal. Start the program with a time of worship. Again, celebrate diversity by having diverse ethnic and denominational traditions represented. Take time to pray around the tables, and have pastors lead prayer from the front. A speaker is not necessary but can be a part of the program if desired.

In September 1997 we held a unity dinner at the Korean Church of Queens. Believers from around the city and neighboring region came for an evening of prayer, praise and fellowship. It was a wonderful opportunity to learn about one another's cultures, pray together, and enjoy both kimchee (a Korean cabbage dish) and Southern-fried chicken.

PRAYER SUMMITS

For eleven years Concerts of Prayer Greater New York has held a Pastors' Prayer Summit every January for two and a half days. The agenda is simply this: to meet with God. There aren't any workshops or keynote speakers, although pastors do share meditations from the Word. The emphasis is on prayer—corporate prayer, small group prayer, individual prayer.

In the 2002 Pastors' Prayer Summit about 300 pastors and ministry leaders gathered at a retreat center in Pennsylvania from Monday noon to Wednesday noon. Many pastors have said the summit is the highlight of their year. Here are some of the comments pastors have shared from recent summits:

"This event sets a good spiritual tone for the whole church in New

York as pastors of many racial backgrounds practice obeying Christ together and overcoming barriers. You will experience great blessings from God by coming together with us in this unique place." Rev. Hi Seon Lee, New Covenant Baptist Church, Queens, N.Y.

"Most of us are called to our own ethnic community. But the Pastors' Prayer Summit affords me the opportunity to transcend my own ethnic community to pray and have fellowship in a multicultural setting, which is ultimately what the body of Christ is all about." Rev. Ray Rivera, Latino Pastoral Action Center, Bronx, N.Y.

"The summit has provided a much needed time to be encouraged and refreshed in the Lord through prayer, worship and fellowship. If you don't come apart, you'll come apart!" Rev. William Sweeting, Leverich Memorial Church, Queens, N.Y.

"The summit is always one of the high points of my year. It is always a time of renewing, refreshing, and most important, refocusing." Rev. Phil Prestamo, First Baptist Church of Freeport, Long Island, N.Y.

"The summit gives me a sense of connectedness and continues adding new dimension to my life spiritually, socially and emotionally." Rev. Jefferson Bannister, Grace Church of God, Brooklyn, N.Y.

"This Pastors' Prayer Summit has been a sign of great hope and light to the New York City area and its surrounding communities. Revival is coming—revival is here!" Rev. Peter Amerman, Hillside Lutheran Church, Penn.

To give you a flavor of how to spend the two or three days in prayer, let me describe our 2002 Pastors' Prayer Summit. The focus was on the book of Ephesians, so the various passages were used as launching points for prayer throughout the summit.

THE MUSIC

Yes, we prayed, but we also sang—a lot. (Hymns and praise songs are often actually prayers directed to the Lord, of course.) A diverse and skilled worship team is vital to an effective summit. Worship leaders lead participants into the presence of God. They are not performers but guides. Strive for a balance of different types of worship songs: include hymns and choruses, songs in English and other languages. Use either an overhead or PowerPoint to project the words, as many may not be familiar with all the songs. Don't sing the songs only once, but repeat them so people have a chance to learn them and begin to focus not on the song itself but on the worship of God. Don't short-change the worship time—spend at least twenty to thirty minutes in worship at the beginning of each prayer time.

THE SCHEDULE

Day 1: At the 2002 summit, pastors and ministry leaders arrived Monday morning, and the first scheduled activity was lunch. The afternoon opening session began with a time of corporate prayer, first by kneeling together and inviting the presence of God. After an extended time of worship, participants prayed around the attributes of God as outlined in Ephesians 1:1-10. Groups of three were formed, and pastors prayed for one another's personal concerns. Many of the spiritual leaders were physically and emotionally exhausted as a result of the tragedy on 9/11. The summit offered a safe place for pastors to share from their hearts and take off the masks

> *"It is not enough for evangelicals merely to participate in the world's affairs and attempt to persuade non-Christians of a right and better way. We must also be people of prayer since we know that apart from God's intervention the world will neither understand nor heed what we are saying."*
>
> JAMES MONTGOMERY BOICE, *TWO CITIES, TWO LOVES*

they often feel compelled to wear in public and at church. With each other, the leaders shared their real concerns, their failures and their dreams.

After dinner on Monday evening, the Rev. David Bryant, founder of Concerts of Prayer International, exhorted the pastors to have a life-style of prayer similar to the calling of the Levites in the Old Testament. Rev. Bryant challenged participants to be prayer activists, vision givers and pace setters. An extended time of prayer was followed by a Communion service. Pastor John Ng, a Chinese pastor, church planter and seminary professor, shared a devotional from Ephesians 2. Pastor Ng said the body of Christ was broken to bring all people together. At the end of his meditation he encouraged everyone to share Communion with someone different from themselves.

Day 2: On Tuesday we fasted. Breakfast and lunch were not served. Juices, coffee and tea were available all day, and plain broth was offered during lunchtime. Pastor Jackson Senyonga shared from Ephesians 3 and talked briefly about the devastation Uganda underwent during the reign of Idi Amin and subsequent dictators, and the transformation now underway in Uganda. The president of Uganda signed a procla-mation dedicating Uganda to God for the next one thousand years! One powerful and visible sign of transformation in Uganda is the reversal of the deadly AIDS trend (it is one of the few countries in the world where the rate of AIDS is declining). The AIDS rate in Uganda has gone from 24 percent in 1991 to 8 percent today! Pastor Senyonga concluded by praying over all assembled that a spirit of intercession would fall on us and drive us into that place of desperation for God.

During the next few hours, after prayer requests were shared from the front, we prayed in small groups for twenty to thirty minutes for each of the stated requests. In the past, we have prayed for the major ethnic groups in New York, for their specific challenges and issues. This year, we prayed thematically: for 9/11 victims, for youth, for those in the marketplace.

We broke the fast with dinner before gathering for our evening meeting. After a brief presentation on the AIDS crisis in Africa, we prayed for those affected—victims, orphans, caregivers, health workers, grandparents, ministers. Informed prayer is significantly more effective than general prayer, so prayer requests were shared from the front, providing everyone with enough specific information to make the prayer time meaningful and valuable.

Day 3: The final morning of the summit was spent praying through the themes found in Ephesians 4—6. We prayed for churches and pastors, for unity in the body of Christ in Metro New York. We prayed for marriages and families, for those we know on the brink of divorce and for sexual purity for ministers. We prayed for the proclamation of the gospel in our great city and around the world.

Without a doubt, the greatest impact of the Pastors' Prayer Summit each year is the creation and deepening of relationships across racial lines. As Latino pastors pray with Korean pastors, and as African American pastors pray with Anglo pastors, they are awakened to the fact that God's church is much bigger than their local church. At the Pastors' Prayer Summit there is a level field: there are no "big church" pastors and "small church" pastors. Everyone who comes is simply a servant of God in need of refreshment, renewal and revival.

THE LORD'S WATCH

The inception of the Lord's Watch in the New York City region was described in chapter four. When we began the Lord's Watch in the New York Metro region in 1995, we asked churches to take one day a month and cover the day with prayer. Churches would designate one day, for example the first Wednesday or the third Friday of the month, and their church members would each sign up for a half-hour or hour of prayer during that twenty-four-hour time period. Over the years we have become a bit more flexible, as we have learned that what works well in some churches doesn't work at all in other churches.

Some churches still choose to take a twenty-four-hour period and have people praying around the clock. Small churches may choose to take a shorter time period, say six or twelve hours, for one day a month. Other churches may pray during a Friday night all-night prayer meeting or during their regular Wednesday night prayer meeting. As we have become less regimented in how the Lord's Watch is conducted, three standards remain:

- Churches must pray *consistently*—at least once a month.
- They must pray *in concert,* unified with the rest of the region by using the monthly prayer guide that is provided.
- They must have a *coordinator.*

One church can start a Lord's Watch, or a whole region can unite in prayer by using the pattern of the Lord's Watch. The Lord's Watch in the Metro New York region has been going strong for seven years. During that time we have experienced ups and downs. Some churches have discontinued their involvement, while other churches have recently joined. It takes commitment and a good coordinator to sustain involvement over a period of time.

HOW TO BEGIN

To start a Lord's Watch in your church or region, you will first need someone who will coordinate it and someone who will write and distribute the monthly prayer guide. Our prayer guide contains requests for each of the four R's (revival, reconciliation, reformation and reaching the lost), listed regionally, nationally and internationally.

Begin by sharing the vision for the Lord's Watch in your church. Meet with the pastor and church leaders, and explain the vision and method for starting a Lord's Watch. A coordinator will be needed to distribute the prayer guide, remind intercessors of their day and hour to pray, and encourage the saints in the work of prayer. Finally, choose a day of the month to pray on, and publicize it in the church.

Once the program catches on in one church, you can invite other churches to observe and imitate your model. Eventually you will have a regional network of churches, together holding their community up to the Lord in prayer.

To recruit people to pray, it is helpful to have a Lord's Watch Sunday. It can be held in one church or in several churches in a region on the same day. Ideally, the sermon on the Lord's Watch Sunday will be on prayer and will end with an appeal for people to sign up to pray during their church's Lord's Watch day.

Sustaining the Lord's Watch requires several important ingredients: a committed coordinator; a prayer guide compiler/writer; a supportive pastor; ongoing regional meetings for training and encouragement; and reports on answered prayer. For more information on how to start and sustain the Lord's Watch in your church or region, or to obtain an explanatory Lord's Watch manual and video, please visit our website at <www.copgny.org>.

NATIONAL DAY OF PRAYER

The National Day of Prayer is held every first Thursday in May. This is the one time of the year when large numbers of believers all across the United States gather at centrally located churches for an evening of unity and prayer. Church affiliations and language barriers lose their significance, and unity takes priority as believers join together in prayer.

In the New York region, pastors begin planning for the National Day of Prayer in January, at the Pastors' Prayer Summit. They meet in regional groups to plan what church or other location they will meet in on the National Day of Prayer. Sometimes pastors choose to use a number of different churches in a borough or county, and sometimes they choose to meet in one central location. In the Bronx, congregations have met at an auditorium in a local college, and they have also met in large churches. They usually have only one site in the Bronx. However, in Queens there are often two or three sites, and some may offer translation in Spanish or Korean.

As pastors from a common region meet together, they decide who will give leadership to the various aspects of the evening of prayer. They identify churches in the region that will be invited to participate, and they schedule one additional planning meeting prior to the National Day of Prayer.

The National Day of Prayer is the only opportunity many believers have to pray with people from other churches in their local community. It is a beautiful expression of oneness in Christ as believers from diverse ethnic, language and denominational backgrounds unite in prayer for one purpose: to glorify God and seek his will and his presence in their city.

CONCERTS OF PRAYER

The phrase "concerts of prayer" was coined by New England revivalist Jonathan Edwards to describe Christians coming together in visible unity and explicit agreement in prayer. A concert of prayer has two primary objectives:

1. to see the body of Christ come together in united prayer

2. to focus on the adoration of Christ, the awakening of Christ's church and the advance of the gospel both locally and globally

Each concert of prayer needs five people in place:

1. The host pastor brings the greeting and introduces the evening.

2. The facilitator or master of ceremonies introduces the various parts of the evening, asks people to form small groups and invites prayer leaders to the pulpit.

3. The worship leader leads worship at the beginning of the evening and throughout the concert of prayer.

4. The "vision giver" highlights the reason for united prayer and the spiritual benefits of united prayer.

5. The offering taker explains the reason for the offering and encourages people to give to offset the costs of the event.

The overall objective is to provide a dynamic experience of united, corporate prayer. It is helpful to recite a statement of unity together, such as the following:

> As we begin this evening of united prayer, we confess our total dependence on God our Father. We confess our total need of the saving work of Jesus Christ. We confess our total reliance on the Holy Spirit who indwells us. We confess our incompleteness without one another. We come from many traditions and prayer styles. We ask, God, that we will appreciate and be sensitive to those who are different from us. We acknowledge our unity in Christ. We can only know the height, depth, breadth, and width of the love of Christ as we know it with all the saints.

Churches may choose to conduct a concert of prayer on their own, or they may connect to the nationally broadcast concert of prayer. The national broadcast is held from 8:00 to 11:00 p.m. EST. Churches will often choose to meet a little earlier, say 7:00 or 7:30, to have some time to pray and worship locally before they join the national broad-

TWO-HOUR CONCERT OF PRAYER
OVERALL THEME: EPHESIANS—GOD'S NEW SOCIETY

✎ ADORATION

Pre-event worship led by diverse worship team	20 minutes
Welcome by host pastor	3 minutes
Facilitator invites people to form small groups for introductions	5 minutes
Worship songs from themes of Ephesians	15 minutes
Scripture reading: Ephesians 1:1-10	2 minutes
People pray in response to God in worship in small groups	5 minutes
Offering—choir sings a selection	5 minutes

✎ AWAKENING

Pastor gives vision for the church	7 minutes
Scripture reading: Ephesians 1:15-22	3 minutes
Prayers of repentance: pastors/leaders pray from the pulpit	10 minutes

    Disunity
    Casualness toward God
    Prayerlessness
    Racism
    Materialism

Small group prayers for the church locally/nationally/ internationally—printed requests provided	10 minutes

✎ ADVANCEMENT

Pastors/leaders pray for the community and nation	10 minutes

    high school and college campuses
    outreach into the marketplace
    the homeless
    AIDS victims
    inmates
    marriages

Prayer in small groups for unbelieving friends and family members	5 minutes
Prayer simultaneously out loud for country of choice	3 minutes

✎ APPLICATION

Pastor gives closing exhortation to be people and churches of prayer	5 minutes
Fill out response forms	5 minutes
Closing Worship	5 minutes
Benediction	2 minutes

Figure 4. A Sample Concert of Prayer Outline

cast. For more information on the nationally broadcast concert of prayer and how to link your church to the broadcast, visit the website <www.concertofprayer.org>. The broadcast links sites across the country into a national prayer meeting. Millions of people across the United States and even Latin America (and worldwide on the Internet) have access to the prayer meeting via satellite either in their local church or at home.

If your church chooses to conduct a local concert of prayer, a two-hour sample outline is offered on page 162.

Whether you are praying from the mountaintop or walking down the streets of Chinatown, whether you pray with five others or five hundred others, God is glorified when his children unite in prayer. A united church at prayer is the most powerful demonstration of the reality of God in the world. When Christians throughout a city pray in unity, we declare our dual citizenship: in the body of Christ, and in the city or town where God has placed us. As we unite in prayer, the barriers of race and culture fall, and we grow into our identity as priests who will one day join the international throng of worshipers from every tribe and tongue in the city of God. Hallelujah!

QUESTIONS FOR REFLECTION OR DISCUSSION

1. Identify at least four "ways to pray."
2. What are some of the benefits of a Pastors' Prayer Summit?
3. Which of the ways to pray would work well in your community?

Next step: Undertake one of the models of prayer identified in this chapter. It can be as simple as prayer-walking in your neighborhood or praying for your pastor during the service on Sunday morning.

10

LEADING OTHERS IN PRAYER
What Happens When Students Pray?

I stood on the platform at Urbana 93, three days after Christmas, and my insides felt as if I was about to jump out of an airplane flying at 20,000 feet. Normally a behind-the-scenes person, this was the largest group I had ever addressed. The Urbana Student Missions Convention is the largest triennial missions gathering in the history of the church, attracting close to 20,000 students, missionaries and ministry leaders every three years at the Urbana campus of the University of Illinois.

This evening was unique: for the first time since InterVarsity began its missions conferences in the 1940s, an entire plenary session was being devoted to a concert of prayer. Brenda Salter McNeil, then an InterVarsity staff member, was the prayer leader in all of the plenary sessions, and I was coleading this evening of prayer with Brenda.

Three themes dominated the evening: worship, service and intercession. Students prayed for countries around the world; for many of them this was the first time they had ever prayed globally. A Japanese student was visibly moved as she heard thousands of other students praying for her country. For many students, it represented the most significant prayer experience in their lifetime.

At the conclusion of the evening, Brenda invited students to stand if they were willing to be prayer leaders on their campuses. Thousands stood and committed themselves to be prayer leaders when they returned. During the remainder of the conference, seminars on leading prayer were standing room only. In the following year, report after report indicated that hundreds of new prayer meetings were springing up on campuses across the United States.

Student prayer has often been the precursor to a great work of God. In 1806, Samuel Mills and four other students at Williams College in Massachusetts prayed under a haystack during a rainstorm. This tiny prayer group committed themselves to world missions before there was a single missions society in North America. Samuel Mills became one of the first missionaries sent out from America.

In 1888, the Student Volunteer Movement was birthed in New York City under the influence of John Mott and Dwight L. Moody. During the next forty years, over 25,000 students were sent around the world as missionaries. In recent years, hundreds of thousands of high school and college students have been awakened to the need for prayer through such initiatives as The Call and See You at the Pole. Only God knows what the fruit of these praying students will be in years to come.

WHAT MAKES A PRAYER MEETING POWERFUL?

Prayer is a mystery—a wonderful mystery. No one can control what God will or won't do, but we do know that God not only commands us to pray, he also desires our communication with him. When I think about that night at Urbana 93, I realize there were a few simple elements that contributed to the powerful impact of the evening on the lives of so many students. The primary elements were:

- elevating worship
- seamless facilitation
- inspiring vision
- honest small group prayer
- an opportunity to respond to God by accepting the challenge to be a prayer mobilizer

Elevating worship. Worship is probably the most qualitative dimension of any spiritual meeting. It is the one thing that God cannot do for himself. Worship is the climactic experience of being centered in the presence of God. Prayer leaders are also worship leaders, and good worship leaders must cultivate and expand their own personal worship experience. Reading the great christological passages in John, Hebrews and Revelation has aided my own experience as a worshiper.

At Urbana 93 the worship team was tremendously gifted musically, but even more important, they had a genuine thirst for worship. A longing for God was evident in their worship, and they acted as musical guides into the presence of God. They were not performing for us; they were communing with God. They were not exulting in the adulation of the audience; they were adoring God.

A good worship team is not just a group of great musicians. A good worship team is a cohesive group that has spent time together, has prayed together and has a common goal: leading others to new heights in worship. At my church, the worship team and choirs go away on at least one retreat a year solely to build stronger relationships with one another.

Good worship feels spontaneous, but it is usually well planned beforehand. At Urbana 93, the worship team had carefully selected songs that reflected the theme of each evening. The words of the songs wove together with the praying and exhortations, all leading to a unified experience of worship and prayer. This is not to say that God cannot change the direction of a worship time—it is always important to allow for the leading of the Spirit and to be flexible and open to change. But having a theme and a direction in mind usually leads to a more significant experience of worship and prayer. This is important whether a prayer meeting has five people or five thousand.

When we think of worship, singing is usually the first thing that we think of, but singing is not the only way to worship God. Reading psalms back to God is a powerful way to worship him. I have been in prayer meetings where people are invited to address to God words from a psalm that emphasizes his attributes. This can go on for several minutes as people encourage one another with truths about God from the Word of God. Another way to worship God is by praying sentences of worship, such as "God, I worship you because . . ." This simple structure is an effective way to encourage everyone to pray and may be comfortable for people who are unused to praying in a group.

Seamless facilitation. Facilitating a prayer meeting is much more of an art than a science. A well-led prayer meeting is as important as a well-preached sermon and should take a similar amount of preparation. When people hear a sermon they hear *about* God, but when they pray they talk *to* God. Both are important to spiritual growth, and both require prayer, forethought and planning.

One of the primary responsibilities of the facilitator is to enable people to connect with one another before they connect with God. They need to feel at home, and people are often ill at ease until they have had a chance to open up and share with someone else. People often wonder if they fit in, or if they are going to say the wrong thing. By sharing in a small group setting commonalities emerge, and as people open up to one another it paves the way for them to open up to God.

I begin most prayer meetings by allowing people to meet one another in small groups of three to six people. I urge people to look for at least one person they don't know—they will always have the opportunity to pray with their friends back at their own church. Once people have formed small groups, I ask them to share three things:

their name, where they are from and something about themselves that most people don't know. People might also be asked to share one thing they would like to see God do in their church or community.

In addition to enabling people to get to know one another, a good facilitator needs to be sensitive to the diversity in the room and able to sensitize the group to the various expressions of worship and prayer. Some people may be accustomed to quiet or even silent praying, while others may come from very expressive, demonstrative backgrounds. Getting folks to understand one another and accept one another's styles is not an easy task, but it must be accomplished for unity to occur. At our first concert of prayer in 1988, a Baptist German brother told me he had a great time, but it was too loud for his liking. A Pentecostal West Indian brother told me he also had a great time, but it was too quiet for him. These two people were at the same meeting but brought different experiences to the gathering and came away with different impressions.

At many of our larger multidenominational prayer gatherings we use a statement of unity at the beginning—something similar to the one in the previous chapter. Stating our mutual dependence on the Lord helps dispel our fears that the person next to us may be feeling spiritually superior to us.

Pastor Senyonga leads many large prayer gatherings with people attending from many different traditions, and he often asks the participants to agree to not be offended. This is an important way to highlight the fact that, though there are differences, in order to maintain relationships that are honoring to God we will not take offense at another's prayer or worship style. Another effective exercise is to have people pair off in twos or in small groups, look at one another and say in unison: "Our praying will be biblical, sensitive and brief." For effect, it helps to pause after *biblical* and *sensitive.*

During a prayer meeting the facilitator may move people in and out of small groups several times. Transitions are extremely important when moving from prayer to singing, to exhortation and back to prayer. The skill with which these transitions are managed will often determine the quality of the prayer experience. It is important that transitions be smoothly managed without abrupt starts and stops.

The facilitator needs to be sensitive to the praying, to the Holy Spirit, but also to the clock. If all the small groups are deep into prayer, even if the clock says it is time to move on, it may not be a good idea to break into the prayer time. Once the praying lets up a little, that is a good time to transition into a song. While people are praying, it helps to have quiet instrumentation in the background to fill in the quiet spaces and promote an atmosphere of prayer. When it is time to transition out of prayer, the facilitator can signal to the pianist or guitarist to begin playing a familiar chorus, and after a couple of minutes to allow people to finish praying, the facilitator or worship leader will lead the group in song.

Inspiring vision. In any prayer gathering it is important for someone to give a short exhortation on the reason for our praying and a vision for the result of our praying. The exhortation is not a full-blown message or sermon but a short, powerful word that articulates why we are praying and to whom. Giving the vision should not take more than seven to ten minutes; it's important to be both passionate and concise!

At Urbana 93, Marilyn Stewart spoke about a call to serve the poor, using John 13 as her text. She and her husband had worked with students in Mexico City, and they had often seen folks who did not have clean water to drink or enough food to eat.

After Marilyn spoke, the prayer time for the poor was very powerful. Marilyn had engaged the hearts and minds of the people as she spoke—she made the object of our praying real. Prayer gave expression to the compassion the students felt after hearing Marilyn's message. As people are preached into prayer, they will pray into revival!

A successful concert of prayer will appear seamless. The singing will give way to the praying, which will be informed by the exhortation. All these elements should reinforce one another and weave together into a unified expression of praise to God.

Honest small group prayer. As mentioned above, at the heart of a corporate prayer gathering is small group praying. Praying can be done corporately, simultaneously, individually and in small groups. But it is in the small group setting where people connect personally with each other as they connect with God. Plan for one or more times when people will break into small groups, pulling chairs into a circle or just standing in a huddle, to hear and lift up each other's concerns. Be sure your instructions from the platform are clear, so everyone will know what to do and no one will feel confused and uncomfortable.

An opportunity to respond. If people enjoy this experience, they will finish up with a longing for more. Clearly offer them a chance to become prayer mobilizers in their own church or community. The power of a praying city comes when lots of people do what they can to get others praying.

TWO TYPES OF INTERCESSION

There are two fundamental types of intercession: "awakening prayer" for the body of Christ and prayer for the world. Both should be part of your corporate prayer events.

Awakening prayer. As we pray for the body of Christ, we are praying that we will "wake up" to the person of Christ and all he is and has for us. Awakening prayer often begins with prayers of personal and corporate confession. One effective way to pray in solidarity is to have people pray out loud in the large group, speaking out one-word phrases that represent areas where we have fallen short. As the whole group maintains an attitude of repentance and prayer, words will echo off one another: *disunity, lust, greed, impatience.* This is a powerful corporate experience of confession.

Guided confession is another way to lead people into repentance. I like to draw from the themes of the Ten Commandments or the "fruit of the Spirit" passage in Galatians 5. A written call/response confession can be printed and included in the program. Here is a sample confessional based on 1 Samuel 7:3-17:

Leader: Samuel could speak to all of Israel because God had all of Samuel.

Congregation: Forgive us where we have been partial in our obedience to you.

Leader: Samuel commanded the Israelites to give up their sexual idolatry.

Congregation: We confess as a people that we have not held to your standards for purity.

Leader: Samuel commanded the Israelites to serve the Lord alone.

Congregation: We confess that we have given in to other competing allegiances.

Leader: God will deliver you from the hand of your enemies.

Congregation: Forgive our unbelief that you have the power to deliver our city and nation.

Leader: Samuel said, "Gather all Israel at Mizpah, and I will pray for you."

Congregation: Forgive our spiritual leaders who have been negligent in calling for prayer.

Leader: The Israelites confessed their sin before the Lord.

Congregation: We too confess that we have sinned as a people in this nation.

Leader: When the people heard of the Philistines, they were afraid of them.

Congregation: Forgive us when we have been marked by fear rather than by your presence.

Leader: The people commanded Samuel to not cease crying out for them.

Congregation: Help us to be a people who cry out to you day and night without ceasing.

Leader: The Lord answered Samuel's cry with loud thunder.

Congregation: We confess that you are able to make yourself unmistakably known in our day.

Leader: Samuel took a stone of remembrance and set it up for all Israel.

Congregation: Help us to look back at this night and see your wonder of deliverance.

Leader: Samuel judged Israel all the days of his life; his house was in Ramah.

Congregation: May we endure all the days of our lives, knowing that our home is with you.

Awakening prayers should include praying for local churches, pastors and ministries. Pray for the unity of the church, for the holiness of the Christian community, for a spirit of evangelism and service, and for a tender heart toward God. We also need to pray for the body of Christ nationally and internationally. Also, pray for Christians in places of influence in the various sectors of culture—education, media, medicine, society, government, economy and religion. Finally, prayers should be made for the international church. Persecution of Christians is rampant in much of the world, notably Muslim and communist countries. Pray for the imprisoned church in China and for the church burying loved ones every day due to the AIDS crisis in Africa.

Prayer for the world. The second kind of praying goes beyond those in the body of Christ; it is prayer for the world. Begin with praying for your friends and family members who have not yet experienced the saving grace of the Lord. Nationally, we need to remember that America is one of the neediest countries in the world, spiritually speaking. Pray for the impact of the gospel to transform our culture. Internationally, there are innumerable spiritual and physical needs that call for prayer. A glance at the newspaper headlines will reveal overwhelming needs: war in the Middle East, the global AIDS crisis, homelessness and poverty, the spiritual needs of those who don't know Christ. The needs are great, so we need to pray.

WHAT'S THE RESULT?

A prayer meeting is not complete without answering the question, so what?

Once people have encountered God and shared their hearts with one another, they will never be the same. Whether it is the weekly church prayer meeting or an annual concert of prayer, people need to be motivated to continue to press on in the work of prayer.

For some it will be a simple resolve to strengthen and lengthen their daily prayer time. Others will be motivated to begin praying with their spouses, children or friends. Some need to be challenged to become prayer leaders and mobilizers in their churches and regions.

At the close of our first concert of prayer in February 1988, an altar call was given for those who felt called to take a leadership role in the burgeoning prayer movement. Bob Bakke came forward. He was then a pastor in northern New Jersey. God lit such a fire in Bob's heart that he began to mobilize prayer in his area immediately on his return to the church. Bob coordinated several Sunday night prayer meetings at William Patterson College; they were filled to capacity. After Bob began to broadcast prayer by radio, he saw the potential for national prayer meetings, and he eventually went to work with the National Day of Prayer broadcast.

For nearly a decade Bob has successfully linked up scores of cities and thousands of churches across the nation by satellite every year on the National Day of Prayer. The spark that was lit in a prayer meeting in Flushing has become a fire of revival as Christians across North and South America are linked up in prayer.

PLANNING A WELL-LED PRAYER MEETING

When you set up a prayer event, plan ahead to be sure every angle of the logistics is covered. Here are some steps you'll need to plan for:

Get people there. The first and greatest need in planning a prayer meeting is simply getting people to show up. Leaders play an important role in motivating people to attend. The best way to motivate others to attend is to demonstrate the importance of the gathering by attending yourself! Instead of simply announcing the prayer meeting, tell the church that you are going and ask people to join you. A recruitment sign-up sheet can be helpful and allows for some accountability. A bulletin insert or sign-up sheet in the lobby after church can serve the same purpose. Announce the prayer meeting several weeks in advance, and give people several opportunities to respond in various ways.

Meet in an appropriate-size room. Almost nothing works against a spirit of prayer more than having a small group of people meet in a large, unfriendly space. Many church meetings are held in a sanctuary where people are drowned in the largely empty space, making them feel weak and small. Yes, God is big and can work anywhere, but from our limited human perspective he inhabits spaces filled with people. Each size group has its strengths. A small group allows for more intimacy, while a large group provides more energy. Whatever the size of the group, try to meet in a room that fits the group. However, don't use a room so small that people don't have the flexibility to move around and turn to pray with others.

When planning a concert of prayer for a church or campus, the host of the event should provide the critical mass. The host church has a leadership role in the event, and as such it should provide from 30-40 people (small to mid-sized churches) to 200-300 people (large churches). When we held a concert of prayer at Greater Allen A.M.E. Cathedral of New York in Jamaica, almost 1,000 church members from Allen itself were present.

Insure that at least 50 percent of the time is spent in prayer. We love to sing, and we love to talk about prayer, but even at prayer meetings we often fail to get to the actual business of praying! Limit the number of people who are speaking, and limit the time they have to speak. A well-led concert of prayer has a theme; without a central unifying theme a prayer meeting will feel disjointed and unsatisfying. Too often leaders speak on their favorite topics and disregard the theme of the prayer meeting. Another danger is for people to speak too long or be unprepared. In order to stimulate effective prayer, good communication between the leader and the speakers must take place before the meeting.

"A failure to pray is not a harmless omission; it is a positive violation of both the self and the society."

EUGENE PETERSON,
EARTH AND ALTAR

One of the powerful aspects of Urbana 93 was the printed prayer requests on all the multimedia screens. Specific prayer requests help people to feel they are praying in agreement. Praying in agreement is powerful. Jesus says that when two or three agree in his name, he is there in their midst. Just imagine his presence in the midst of two hundred people praying, or two thousand people praying.

Think through leadership positions. A concert of prayer or other city-wide prayer initiative should minimally include the following leadership positions: host, facilitator/MC; worship leader; vision giver; closing challenge giver. In addition, pastors and spiritual leaders will need to be involved prior to the event to give input and encourage people to attend. Each role should be identified in advance, with expectations clearly understood by all involved. Additional leadership positions can include Scripture readers and prayer leaders (who pray from the podium). At least one advance meeting will be needed for the leadership to meet and plan out the prayer gathering.

Anticipate follow-up plans. Too often all the effort for a prayer meeting goes into the planning of the event itself, and follow-through is not anticipated or planned for. Before any prayer gathering takes place, it's important to answer the question, How will we sustain the momentum in prayer? Effective follow-up may include response forms, an invitation to subsequent prayer gatherings, training for potential prayer leaders, encouragement to form pastors' or lay people's prayer groups. What happens after the gathering is almost as important as what happens during the gathering, and that needs to be anticipated and planned in advance.

In New York we have a rhythm of prayer events that feed into each other and provide for continuity. Pastors unite at the Pastors' Prayer Summit in January; prayer leaders come together at the Lord's Watch training event in March; and the whole body of Christ unites in May on the National Day of Prayer.

RETURN TO URBANA

One of the highlights of my life was leading my second concert of prayer at Urbana in 1996. The focus was on the cities of the world, and a woman who is a missionary in Egypt spoke at the plenary session. Rebecca Atallah works among the desperately poor of Cairo, who collect and sort garbage to try to make a living—and who comprise the largest congregation in the city. They meet in a cave amphitheater that seats over 10,000 people. It's the largest church in the Middle East! We prayed for Cairo, Tokyo and New York City.

As we closed the evening, I held up a copy of a *New York Times* article from December 20, 1996, that highlighted the 70 percent drop in the murder rate in New York City over a three-year period. It was a dramatic reminder that the work of prayer is participating with God in the transformation of our cities.

My own journey to New York began at Urbana 79 as a college student. Seventeen years later I led a congregation of 20,000 to pray for New York City. Amazingly, God took a banker's son from South Dakota and brought me into leadership in the prayer movement in New York City. Where is God calling you?

177

QUESTIONS FOR REFLECTION OR DISCUSSION

1. Why is it helpful to share in small groups before praying together?
2. Why is planning so important to a good prayer meeting?
3. What ingredients listed in this chapter for planning and leading a prayer meeting would be helpful to incorporate into your own church prayer meeting?

Next step: Share some of the lessons you have learned in this chapter with prayer leaders in your church.

11

WHEN GOD SHOWS UP

In the summer of 1858, Fifth Avenue in Manhattan was not crowded with taxis. High-end stores like Saks Fifth Avenue did not line the wide street. Horse and buggy was the primary mode of transportation when the cornerstone of St. Patrick's Cathedral was laid before a cheering crowd of over 100,000 people. With years of labor the spires soared into the sky, and twenty-one years later, on Sunday, May 25, 1879, the cathedral was dedicated to God.

The Irish wanted to build this grand cathedral to house the worship of a majestic God. Thankful to be alive, these immigrants had left a country devastated by the potato famine—over a million emigrated during the famine in the 1840s, and another million died of starvation and disease. St. Patrick's stands today as a symbol of American Catholicism and a monument to the determination of a devastated people to worship God in their new land.

GOD SPEAKS TO A LEADER

King David wanted to build a grand temple for God. His vision was not unlike that of the Irish Catholics: he wanted to build a magnificent structure as a tribute to the King of Glory, the Lord Almighty, the Rock of Ages. But God wouldn't allow his servant David to build the temple.

> King David rose to his feet and said, "Listen to me, my brothers and my people. I had it in my heart to build a house as a place of rest for the ark of the covenant of the Lord, for the footstool of our God, and

I made plans to build it. But God said to me, 'You are not to build a house for my Name, because you are a warrior and have shed blood.' "
(1 Chron 28:2-3)

Although David was not permitted to build the temple, God chose David's son Solomon to build it. God told David, "Solomon your son is the one who will build my house and my courts, for I have chosen him to be my son, and I will be his father" (1 Chron 28:6). King David urged his son to follow God wholeheartedly, gave Solomon the architectural plans for the temple and provided all the resources necessary to accomplish the task. David was determined to have the temple built, even if it didn't happen in his lifetime.

After Solomon was established as king, he assembled all Israel before him: commanders, judges, leaders, heads of families. They all went up to the high place at Gibeon, to a makeshift temple, the Tent of Meeting. Solomon offered a thousand burnt offerings to God on the bronze altar at Gibeon—a picture of extravagant worship and praise to God. That night God appeared to Solomon and said, "Ask for whatever you want me to give you" (2 Chron 1:7). Solomon worshiped God with all his heart, and God responded by offering to give Solomon his heart's desire.

Solomon set the stage for his humble request by acknowledging God's grace and dominion, mentioning that God had showed kindness to his father, David, and that the people of Israel belonged to God. With this perspective, Solomon formed his request. What he didn't ask for is almost as important as what he did ask for. Solomon didn't ask for wealth, riches or honor; he didn't ask for the heads of his enemies or a long life; he didn't ask for a large army or more power. Solomon asked for wisdom and knowledge—wisdom to lead God's people.

Because Solomon worshiped God and came before him humbly,

God responded by promising Solomon not only what he asked for but also much, much more. God promised, "Wisdom and knowledge will be given you. And I will also give you wealth, riches and honor, such as no king who was before you ever had and none after you will have" (2 Chron 1:12). The renewal of the nation of Israel began when God spoke to Solomon. The renewal of our nation, our churches and our cities begins when God speaks to our spiritual leaders.

Seven Years of Searching, One Night of Conversion

A. R. Bernard was a successful banker in the mid-seventies, but he was spiritually bankrupt. God broke through to him on January 11, 1975, through evangelist Nicky Cruz. (Nicky Cruz was the notorious gang leader of the violent Mau Maus until he heard the message of the gospel. In the past forty years, Nicky has ministered to thousands of inner-city gang members as he speaks to their need from his own experience.) That Saturday night in January, Nicky gave his testimony and clearly explained the gospel. A. R. Bernard's seven-year search for a Savior ended as he heard God speak to him clearly: "I am the God you are looking for. I and my word are one."[1]

A. R. Bernard had gotten involved with many different spiritual expressions—Buddhism, Hinduism, witchcraft, Nation of Islam—during his seven-year spiritual hunt for truth. He felt pulled to the Nation of Islam because "they symbolized strength and order and provided an opportunity for the community of color to resolve its identity crisis." Then God used two unlikely vessels: a Spanish Pentecostal coworker, who invited A. R. to church, and a former gang leader, Nicky Cruz, who led him to Christ.

Just three years after his conversion, A. R. Bernard felt called to the ministry and was ordained by the Church of God in Christ. His first church grew out of a Bible study that met at the bank. That storefront church in Brooklyn was beginning a twenty-five-year journey of growing into what is now the 15,000-member Christian Cultural Center. Rev. Bernard took his profit sharing out of the bank and invested it in the church. Using wood that he bought himself, he built the first platform and podium with his own hands. Starting out in the ministry, there were no guarantees and very little money; times were hard.

There were times when the church lights stayed on but the lights at home went out. With three sons and a wife to support, sometimes the week stretched longer than the pay, and the whole family lived on turkey necks and chicken backs. Rev. Bernard remembers a time when "we had no money or food, and a church member brought over fifteen pounds of hot dogs." For the next two weeks they learned how to make hot dogs in a variety of creative ways—boiled, baked, grilled, barbecued, chopped and fried!

Like Solomon, Rev. Bernard was called by God to lead his people, and like Solomon, Rev. Bernard sacrificed to become the leader God was calling him to be.

SOLOMON BUILDS THE TEMPLE

King Solomon gave orders to build the temple, deploying 153,000 workers to complete the massive task. Solomon sent a message to the King of Tyre, Hiram, asking for cedar logs. Solomon explained to Hiram, "The temple I am going to build will be great, because our God is greater than all other gods" (2 Chron 2:5). Solomon acknowledged that no temple could actually hold God, "since the heavens, even the highest heavens, cannot contain him" (2 Chron 2:6). The temple would be the place to worship God, to offer sacrifices to him—and Solomon wanted it to be magnificent and beautiful.

Hiram responded to Solomon's request by saying, "Because the Lord loves his people, he has made you their king" (2 Chron 2:11). What a testimony to the reputation of Solomon! Hiram affirmed Solomon's leadership and agreed to send the resources and the skilled labor needed for the project.

During the next seven years the temple was built, on the very site where Abraham had gone to sacrifice Isaac in obedience to God. Every detail was attended to, every aspect carefully constructed, from the foundation to the ceiling, from the curtains to the altar, from the entrance to the Most Holy Place.

The temple represented God dwelling with his people. The symbols inside the temple represented the holiness of God and the mercy of God. Solomon built the temple so that the people of God would have a proper setting to experience the presence of God.

BUILDING THE CHURCH

Rev. Bernard didn't stay at that little storefront in Brooklyn. As his small congregation grew, he had to keep finding larger and larger spaces for the Christian Life Centre, as it was then called. From the storefront they moved to a second floor loft; from the loft they moved to the Automotive High School auditorium; from the high school they moved to a Days Inn Motel in Manhattan; from the motel they moved to a Salvation Army building on 14th Street in Manhattan. You get the picture—continual growth and continual moving.

Christian Life Centre was holding four services when Rev. Bernard began to dream about building a church that would hold the entire burgeoning congregation, although he knew it would not hold their awesome God! Finally, in 1989, they were able to purchase a Key

Food supermarket and begin converting it into a church. Then, ten years after they purchased the supermarket, a brand new building was erected to hold the congregation, now numbering in the thousands.

The new building is named the Christian Cultural Center. In 1986 Rev. Bernard became convinced that the purpose of Christianity is to bring forth a new culture, not become integrated into existing cultures. Rev. Bernard believes that when God gave the Ten Commandments "his objective was to give a body of law upon which a proper sociological structure could be built. It is not a great race that makes a great culture, but a great social order." Rev. Bernard teaches his members what it means to embrace Christianity as a culture, and in 2003 the Christian Cultural Center will open a museum dedicated to showcasing the history of Christianity.

Of the 15,000 members of the Christian Cultural Center, about 48 percent are men. This is unusual in any church, but even more rare in a church made up predominantly of people of color. Rev. Bernard and his wife have done their share to add to the male population of the church—they have seven sons! Rev. Bernard's messages about right priorities, integrity, character, balance and leadership are the main ingredients to personal as well as church growth. His emphasis on instructing men to disciple their families has put men and the family back in the position God intended.[2]

The temple (in this case the Center) is an expression of the presence of God in the midst of a city, and it is a testimony to the leadership of a man devoted to God. On Sunday mornings the congregation spends about an hour in worship. Congregants are led into the presence of God by a small but dynamic worship team, and they linger in the presence of God in extended worship and prayer. The congregation is about 90 percent people of color—African American, Caribbean,

Central and South American, Asian and African—but there are white faces sprinkled throughout the sanctuary as well.

The 4,800-seat sanctuary, built like a theater complete with three large screens, is one of the largest in New York City. On October 11, the one-month anniversary of the tragedy at the World Trade Center and the Pentagon, the Christian Cultural Center hosted a memorial service. The service included the testimony of four New York Yankees (via video), the testimony of a widow (who was eight months pregnant), and messages from Rev. Franklin Graham and Rev. A. R. Bernard. The memorial service galvanized Christian leaders in the region to express in unity a response to the city and the country from Ground Zero. Just as God used Solomon to lead his people and to build his temple, God is using Rev. Bernard and countless other ministers to lead his people and build his church today.

God called Dan Mercaldo to be a leader and a builder when he was just twelve years old. It was 1951, and Dan had a serious case of polio that the doctors predicted would kill him. The doctors left him to die, but the church prayed through the night. On Wednesday, September 5, Dan asked God to spare his life. He promised God that if he lived, he would give up his dream of replacing Pee Wee Reese on the Brooklyn Dodgers and would live to serve God.

God did spare his life, and fifty-one years later Pastor Dan Mercaldo is still leading the people of God and still building! He has pastored Gateway Cathedral on Staten Island since 1965. Starting with just sixteen members, the church has outgrown several buildings and is now in the process of constructing a 3,000-seat cathedral. On twenty-three acres of land near the gateway to New York City, the Verrazano Narrows Bridge, Gateway Cathedral encompasses an 800-seat sanctuary built in 1990, a Christian school with 200 students and a thriving theological education program.

Pastor Mercaldo describes himself as a builder. But he doesn't just build buildings. He is called by God to build strong families and to build a strong prayer life in the church.

Gateway Cathedral is one of the strongest Lord's Watch churches in the city, with over 135 people signed up to pray for a half-hour to an hour once a month. Every Sunday, Pastor Dan prays for all the pastors he knows. As the buildings have been erected, the church has been built on prayer.

THE FIRE FALLS: WORSHIP AND PRAYER

Once the temple was completed, Solomon assembled Israel once again and brought the ark of the Lord into the Most Holy Place. The priests consecrated themselves, and Levitical musicians played their harps, cymbals and lyres, accompanied by 120 priests sounding trumpets. "The trumpeters and singers joined in unison, as with one voice, to give praise and thanks to the Lord" (2 Chron 5:13). Can you picture it? Singing, playing, praying—all ascending to the throne of God. Worship.

God's presence was in their midst. The temple was filled with a cloud so thick that the priests could not even see well enough to perform their priestly duties. Against this backdrop of glory and worship, Solomon paused to pray. It is the longest recorded prayer in the Bible. Solomon prayed that God would hear their prayer, heal their land and forgive their sins. He emphasized the importance of the name of God, representing the essence of God's person and character. Solomon mentioned the "name" of God fourteen times in his prayer. He reminded God that his own name was at stake and that the reputation of God's name was bound up in the welfare of God's people. Solomon understood that there is no hope apart from a prayer-answering God.

As Solomon finished praying, fire came down from heaven and consumed the burnt offering. The glory of the Lord filled the temple. As the fire came down, the Israelites too came down—they knelt down on the pavement with their faces to the ground. As God manifested his presence in the temple, Solomon sacrificed 22,000 cattle and 120,000 sheep and goats. The sacrifice was an overwhelming sensory experience, bringing the aroma of worship before the presence of God. In that environment of worship, Solomon and the nation dedicated the temple to God. The celebration continued for fourteen days.

Solomon demonstrated the principles of spiritual leadership. He met with God and led the people into the presence of God. He deployed the finest and best resources to build the temple. Most important, Solomon prayed. He asked God to dwell in the temple he had built. God responded to Solomon's humility, his perseverance, his sacrifice and his prayer. God made himself unmistakably known in the midst of the nation.

Pastor Bob Johansson has learned the principles of spiritual leadership in his forty-year ministry in Queens, New York, and he has learned the power of prayer. He is the pastor of Evangel Church, which was founded by his grandfather. As the little church began to grow, Pastor Johansson dreamed of building a church, a cathedral, for the worship of God. He had a vision. As the church grew from a few hundred to a few thousand people, a building was needed to accommodate the growth.

Evangel Church met in many facilities as it grew over the years. Finally enough money was raised to begin work on the church building.

The church Pastor Johansson envisioned had lots of windows. He wanted the sunlight to shine in on worshipers as a reminder that Jesus is the Light of the World. The church would have fine wood; he made plans for beautiful oak pews and finishing, in contrast to the concrete city. The church would be spacious, an antidote to the crowded conditions of city life. Like David and Solomon, Pastor Johansson wanted a magnificent temple for the people of God to come to in worship and prayer.

"Prayer leads you to see new paths and to hear new melodies in the air. Prayer is the breath of your life which gives you freedom to go and stay where you wish and to find the many signs which point out the way to a new land."

HENRI NOUWEN, *WITH OPEN HANDS*

The first service in the new sanctuary was Easter Sunday 1998. During the call to worship, members carried native flags from eighty-two countries as they processed to the altar. Someone representing the risen Christ sat on a makeshift throne. As the first person in the processional reached the stage, the procession stopped. In silent reverence, all the flag bearers knelt down in worship with their flags, signifying all nations bowing down to the Lord Jesus Christ.

That moment was worth thirty-five years of ministry; it was worth the struggles, the obstacles, the sacrifice. In that moment of extravagant worship, Pastor Johansson saw the fulfillment of a lifelong dream of building on his grandfather's foundation and leading the people of God—just as Solomon built on the foundation laid by his father David.

To what does he attribute the growth of the church? To prayer. At Evangel Church prayer is a priority. One group of intercessors prays for the pastors weekly; another group meets to pray for the work of the urban ministry. Evangel is a strong Lord's Watch church, under the direction of coordinator Aida Force. There are nearly two hundred people praying around the clock every first Friday and Saturday. Prayer has opened the hearts of the people to God and allowed God to pour out his blessings on the people.

Rev. Bernard also knows the power of prayer. He calls prayer "the sinew that holds us together." He credits the growth of the Christian Cultural Center—from its humble beginnings in 1978 to its current membership of over 15,000—to prayer. Prayer is where the power is. Rev. Bernard teaches that prayer is an integral part of the daily walk of every believer. There is someone praying for the Christian Cultural Center's ministry twenty-four hours a day, seven days a week.

> *Prayer is "the sinew that holds us together."*
>
> A. R. BERNARD

United prayer is what explains the presence of God in a church, in a city or in a nation. Rev. Bernard believes that "prayer opens the space in human society for God to enter." God has given us human will, and he tells us to ask him when we need something. "The asking is the engaging of our will which gives him permission to intervene in human society. That is the power of prayer."

THE LORD APPEARS TO SOLOMON

After the dedication of the temple, boundless worship and desperate prayer, Solomon retires to his palace, and once again the Lord appears to him. God reassures Solomon, "I have heard your prayer and have chosen this place for myself as a temple for sacrifices" (2 Chron 7:12). The building of the temple was not in vain. God is pleased to dwell in the temple among his people.

God responds to Solomon using the same language Solomon used as he prayed. God promises that when his people humble themselves (as Solomon did), pray and seek his face (as Solomon did), and turn from their wicked ways, he will hear, forgive and heal. What a glorious promise! As the people of God cry out to God, he hears, he forgives, and he heals not just us but our land. *That is the power of a city at prayer.*

The power is in God's hands as he is asked, as he is given permission, to enter into the city. As believers unite in prayer and ask God to hear, forgive and heal, God will respond. God dwells in the midst of his people. Just as the fire came down when the Israelites were worshiping God in the temple they had built to his name, God will send down the fire of his presence when his people unite in prayer and worship.

God can dwell in a city without magnificent cathedrals. He meets his children when they talk with him from a park bench, a prison cell, a kitchen table, a storefront church. But these buildings are a testimony to the majesty of God. They proclaim the presence of God, and they declare the determination of God's people to worship him in the places of the earth to which he has called them. So rejoice that the Irish Catholics built St. Patrick's Cathedral. Rejoice that in Brooklyn over 15,000 people come to worship at the Christian Cultural Center. Rejoice that Christians from 82 different countries worship every Sunday at Evangel Church. Rejoice that at the gateway to the city, Gateway Cathedral stands in Staten Island as a testimony to the grace of God. Rejoice in these temples made by humans to house the worship of our God and King! For as the people of God come to worship and to pray, the power of a city at prayer is manifest: God's power is unleashed in the city, in the nation and around the world.

QUESTIONS FOR REFLECTION OR DISCUSSION

1. What did Solomon ask God for, and what did God give him?
2. Why are temples and churches important to the people of God?
3. What is the power of a city at prayer?

Next step: Pray about how you will incorporate what you have learned in this book into your life.

Notes

Chapter 2: Pentecost to Prayer Mountain
[1]John R. W. Stott, *The Spirit, the Church and the World* (Downers Grove, Ill.: InterVarsity Press, 1990), p. 68.
[2]Ibid., p. 293.
[3]Catherine O. Sweeting, "This Far by Faith," in Robert D. Carle and Louis A. DeCaro Jr., eds., *Signs of Hope in the City* (Valley Forge, Penn.: Judson Press, 1999), p. 80.

Chapter 3: Five Dimensions of Prayer
[1]Pastor Jackson Senyonga's four prerequisites are taken from a talk he gave on March 8, 2002, at New York Presbyterian Church in Long Island City, Queens.
[2]Ken Gire, *Reflections on Your Life Journal* (Colorado Springs, Colo.: Cook Communications Ministries, 1998), p. 8.

Chapter 4: Transforming Prayer for a Broken City
[1]Robert D. Carle and Louis A. DeCaro Jr., eds., *Signs of Hope in the City* (Valley Forge, Penn.: Judson Press, 1991), p. 115.
[2]Ibid., p. 117.
[3]Ibid., p. 111.

Chapter 5: Raising Up a Prayer Leader
[1]Max DePree, *Leadership Is an Art* (New York: Dell, 1989), p. 11.

Chapter 7: For All the Saints
[1]All direct quotes from David Bryant were obtained in an interview conducted by Katie Sweeting on March 13, 2002.
[2]John R. W. Stott, *God's New Society* (Downers Grove, Ill.: InterVarsity Press, 1980), p. 69.
[3]Ibid., pp. 111-12.
[4]Ibid., p. 126.
[5]Ibid., pp. 126-29.
[6]Ibid., p. 123.

Chapter 8: Being a Servant Leader
[1]From an interview with Jeremy Del Rio conducted by Katie Sweeting on February 27, 2002.
[2]Barnabas was a Levite, and although Levites did not own land in Palestine, Barnabas could have owned land as he lived in Cyprus. Or if he was married, the land sold could have been his wife's property.

[3]Abounding Grace Church, Rev. Richard Del Rio, pastor (see chapter one for more on Rev. Del Rio).

[4]See <www.generationxcel.com>.

[5]John R. W. Stott, *The Spirit, the Church and the World* (Downers Grove, Ill.: InterVarsity Press, 1990), p. 178.

[6]Ibid., p. 205.

[7]Charles W. Colson, *Born Again* (Lincoln, Va.: Chosen Books, 1976), p. 133.

[8]Ibid., p. 146.

[9]Ibid., p. 150.

Chapter 9: Some Ways to Pray
[1]C. Peter Wagner, *Churches That Pray* (Ventura, Calif.: Regal, 1993), pp. 169-70.

Chapter 11: When God Shows Up
[1]All quotes from Rev. Bernard are from an interview conducted by Katie Sweeting on April 4, 2002.

[2]From <www.clc.org> website.

A portion of the authors' proceeds from this book will go to support AIDS ministry in New York City through Bruised Reed Ministry (BruisedReedMin@aol.com) and in Africa through World Vision (www.worldvision.org).